THIRD EDITION

3

Skills for Success
READING AND WRITING

Colin S. Ward | Margot F. Gramer

OXFORD
UNIVERSITY PRESS

OXFORD
UNIVERSITY PRESS

198 Madison Avenue
New York, NY 10016 USA

Great Clarendon Street, Oxford, OX2 6DP, United Kingdom

Oxford University Press is a department of the University of Oxford.
It furthers the University's objective of excellence in research, scholarship,
and education by publishing worldwide. Oxford is a registered trade
mark of Oxford University Press in the UK and in certain other countries

ISBN: 978 0 19 490394 3   Student Book 3 with iQ Online pack
ISBN: 978 0 19 490370 7   Student Book 3 as pack component
ISBN: 978 0 19 490430 8   iQ Online student website

Printed in China

This book is printed on paper from certified and well-managed sources

ACKNOWLEDGEMENTS

Back cover photograph: Oxford University Press building/David Fisher

Illustrations by: Karen Minot p.32

*The Publishers would like to thank the following for their kind permission to reproduce
photographs and other copyright material*:

Alamy: pp.27 (woman presenting to colleagues/Hero Images Inc.),
43 (Chinese restaurant/Edward Herdwick), 73 (man crossing road/
SiliconValleyStock), 80 (Times Square/Alexander Spatari), 84 (woman
shopping/Phanie), 95 (social media login page/LondonPhotos - Homer
Sykes), 112 (children in front of shack/imagebroker), 185 (woman weaving
basket/Jake Lyell); Getty: Cover (Alfon No/500px Prime), pp.2 (man
presenting to group/Caiaimage/TomMerton), 5 (small talk/Caiaimage/Paul
Bradbury), 6 (businessmen shaking hands/Caiaimage/Paul Bradbury), 18
(family greeting/Hero Images), 28 (chef plating up food/Carlos Sanchez
Pereyra), 31 (woman pulling sour face/Eva-Katalin), 54 (girl in basket
with cellphone/Bloomberg), 58 (driverless car/Chesky_W), 64 (children
working on tablets/PeopleImages), 83 (couple in a restaurant/10'000
Hours), 88 (bus advertisement/Richard Baker / Contributor), 104 (man
running with prosthetic/MichaelSvoboda), 107 (girl being introduced to
class/Niedring/Drentwett), 108 (man in front of devastated house/David
DUCOIN / Contributor), 130 (boy choosing a skateboard/Sigrid Gombert),
136 (students running up steps/XiXinXing), 145 (business people around
a table/Thomas Barwick), 157 (mother and daughter choosing cakes/
Hero Images), 162 (FEED bags/Astrid Stawiarz / Stringer), 173 (group
of people with plant saplings/PeopleImages), 186 (women celebrating
ascent of mountain/swissmediavision), 210 (football team celebrating
success/Hero Images); OUP: pp.65 (façade of Petra/Shutterstock/Yongyut
Kumsri), 103 (hot air balloons/Shutterstock / Twin Design), 134 (student
thinking/wavebreakmedia), 146 (firefighters tackling a blaze/Shutterstock/
Johnny Habell), 175 (black rhino/Shutterstock/AndChisPhoto), 194
(woman running/Shutterstock/Daxiao Productions);   Shutterstock: pp.13
(video conference/fizkes), 16 (woman in job interview/Lucky Business),
38 (attractive dish of food/Ricardo Villasenor), 39 (dessert on plate/
Andreshkova Nastya), 53 (food hall in Thailand/Steve Allen), 57 (man in
driverless car/Scharfsinn), 65 (POV taking photo on cellphone/tanatat), 69
(buying online with credit card/Worawee Meepian), 79 (airport checkin
kiosks/i viewfinder), 84 (hiking boot/Cultura Motion), 90 (woman in café/
ShutterOK), 116 (climbers on Half Dome mountain/Mark Yarchoan), 117
(Half Dome/klarka0608), 120 (person on galloping horse/NiP STUDIO), 129
(people repairing a damaged roof/Str/EPA), 133 (people waiting for elevator/
Dragon Images), 180 (sunflower in field/Matt Kremkau), 189 (F1 car/
Jens Mommens), 190 (F1 driver/cristiano barni), 195 (young boys playing
soccer/Fotokostic), 199 (university football team/Keeton Gale), 201 (boys
playing soccer in playground/sunsinger); Third party: pp.84 (Adchoice logo/
Adchoice), 158 (eyeglasses being fitted to man/VisionSpring@Bangladesh),
161 (Lauren Bush Lauren handing out a school meal/FEED Projects), 168
(children wearing TOMS shoes/TOMS shoes), 169 (children with Nokero
lights/Nokero Solar), 171 (woman fitting girl with shoe/TOMS shoes).

*The authors and publisher are grateful to those who have given permission to
reproduce the following extracts and adaptations of copyright material:*

p. 90 From 'In Defense of Advertising' by Terry O'Reilly and Mike Tennant,
from The Age of Persuasion Radio Show, CBC radio, broadcast April 26,
2008, www.cbc.ca. Reproduced by permission.

p. 107 From 'How People Learn to Become Resilient' by Maria Konnikova,
11 February, 2016. The New Yorker © Condé Nast. Reproduced by
permission.

p. 116 Extract from 'The Climb of My Life: Scaling Mountains with a
Borrowed Heart' by Kelly Perkins, 2007, Rowman and Littlefield Publishers.
Reproduced by permission of Kelly Perkins.

Although every effort has been made to trace and contact copyright
holders before publication, this has not been possible in some cases. We
apologize for any apparent infringement of copyright and if notified, the
publisher will be pleased to rectify any errors or omissions at the earliest
opportunity.

Sources: p. 161 www.forbes.com, www.feedprojects.com

We would like to acknowledge the teachers from all over the world who participated in the development process and review of *Q: Skills for Success* Third Edition.

USA

Kate Austin, Avila University, MO; **Sydney Bassett**, Auburn Global University, AL; **Michael Beamer**, USC, CA; **Renae Betten**, CBU, CA; **Pepper Boyer**, Auburn Global University, AL; **Marina Broeder**, Mission College, CA; **Thomas Brynmore**, Auburn Global University, AL; **Britta Burton**, Mission College, CA; **Kathleen Castello**, Mission College, CA; **Teresa Cheung**, North Shore Communtiy College, MA; **Shantall Colebrooke**, Auburn Global University, AL; **Kyle Cooper**, Troy University, AL; **Elizabeth Cox**, Auburn Global University, AL; **Ashley Ekers**, Auburn Global University, AL; **Rhonda Farley**, Los Rios Community College, CA; **Marcus Frame**, Troy University, AL; **Lora Glaser**, Mission College, CA; **Hala Hamka**, Henry Ford College, MI; **Shelley A. Harrington**, Henry Ford College, MI; **Barrett J. Heusch**, Troy University, AL; **Beth Hill**, St. Charles Community College, MO; **Patty Jones**, Troy University, AL; **Tom Justice**, North Shore Community College, MA; **Robert Klein**, Troy University, AL; **Wheeler Loreley**, North Shore Communtiy College, MA; **Patrick Maestas**, Auburn Global University, AL; **Elizabeth Merchant**, Auburn Global University, AL; **Rosemary Miketa**, Henry Ford College, MI; **Myo Myint**, Mission College, CA; **Lance Noe**, Troy University, AL; **Irene Pannatier**, Auburn Global University, AL; **Annie Percy**, Troy University, AL; **Erin Robinson**, Troy University, AL; **Juliane Rosner**, Mission College, CA; **Mary Stevens**, North Shore Communtiy College, MA; **Pamela Stewart**, Henry Ford College, MI; **Karen Tucker**, Georgia Tech, GA; **Amanda Wilcox**, Auburn Global University, AL; **Heike Williams**, Auburn Global University, AL

Canada

Angelika Brunel, Collège Ahuntsic, QC; **David Butler**, English Language Institute, BC; **Paul Edwards**, Kwantlen Polytechnic University, BC; **Cody Hawver**, University of British Columbia, BC; **Olivera Jovovic**, Kwantlen Polytechnic University, BC; **Tami Moffatt**, Univeristy of British Columbia, BC; **Dana Pynn**, Vancouver Island University, BC

Latin America

Georgette Barreda, SENATI, Peru; **Claudia Cecilia Díaz Romero**, Colegio América, Mexico; **Jeferson Ferro**, Uninter, Brazil; **Mayda Hernández**, English Center, Mexico; **Jose Ixtaccihusatl**, Tecnologico de Tecomatlan, Mexico; **Andreas Paulus Pabst**, CBA Idiomas, Brazil; **Amanda Carla Pas**, Instituição de Ensino Santa Izildinha, Brazil; **Allen Quesada Pacheco**, University of Costa Rica, Costa Rica; **Rolando Sánchez**, Escuela Normal de Tecámac, Mexico; **Luis Vasquez**, CESNO, Mexico

Asia

Asami Atsuko, Women's University, Japan; **Rene Bouchard**, Chinzei Keiai Gakuenj, Japan; **Francis Brannen**, Sangmyoung University, South Korea; **Haeyun Cho**, Songang University, South Korea; **Daniel Craig**, Sangmyoung University, South Korea; **Thomas Cuming**, Royal Melbourne Institute of Technology, Vietnam; **Jissen Joshi Daigaku**, Women's University, Japan; **Nguyen Duc Dat**, OISP, Vietnam; **Wayne Devitte**, Tokai University, Japan; **James D. Dunn**, Tokai University, Japan; **Fergus Hann**, Tokai University, Japan; **Michael Hood**, Nihon University College of Commerce, Japan; **Hideyuki Kashimoto**, Shijonawate High School, Japan; **David Kennedy**, Nihon University, Japan; **Anna Youngna Kim**, Songang University, South Korea; **Jae Phil Kim**, Songang University, South Korea; **Jaganathan Krishnasamy**, GB Academy, Malaysia; **Peter Laver**, Incheon National University, South Korea; **Hung Hoang Le**, Ho Chi Minh City University of Technology, Vietnam; **Hyon Sook Lee**, Songang University, South Korea; **Ji-seon Lee**, Iruda English Institute, South Korea; **Joo Young Lee**, Songang University, South Korea; **Phung Tu Luc**, Ho Chi Minh City University of Technology, Vietnam; **Richard Mansbridge**, Hoa Sen University, Vietnam; **Kahoko Matsumoto**, Tokai University, Japan; **Elizabeth May**, Sangmyoung University, South Korea; **Naoyuki Naganuma**, Tokai University, Japan; **Hiroko Nishikage**, Taisho University, Japan; **Yongjun Park**, Sangji University, South Korea; **Paul Rogers**, Dongguk University, South Korea; **Scott Schafer**, Inha University, South Korea; **Michael Schvaudner**, Tokai University, Japan; **Brendan Smith**, RMIT University, School of Languages and English, Vietnam; **Peter Snashall**, Huachiew Chalermprakiat University, Thailand; **Makoto Takeda**, Sendai Third Senior High School, Japan; **Peter Talley**, Mahidol University, Faculty of ICT, Thailand; **Byron Thigpen**, Songang University, South Korea; **Junko Yamaai**, Tokai University, Japan; **Junji Yamada**, Taisho University, Japan; **Sayoko Yamashita**, Women's University, Japan; **Masami Yukimori**, Taisho University, Japan

Middle East and North Africa

Sajjad Ahmad, Taibah University, Saudi Arabia; **Basma Alansari**, Taibah University, Saudi Arabia; **Marwa Al-ashqar**, Taibah University, Saudi Arabia; **Dr. Rashid Al-Khawaldeh**, Taibah University, Saudi Arabia; **Mohamed Almohamed**, Taibah University, Saudi Arabia; **Dr Musaad Alrahaili**, Taibah University, Saudi Arabia; **Hala Al Sammar**, Kuwait University, Kuwait; **Ahmed Alshammari**, Taibah University, Saudi Arabia; **Ahmed Alshamy**, Taibah University, Saudi Arabia; **Doniazad sultan AlShraideh**, Taibah University, Saudi Arabia; **Sahar Amer**, Taibah University, Saudi Arabia; **Nabeela Azam**, Taibah University, Saudi Arabia; **Hassan Bashir**, Edex, Saudi Arabia; **Rachel Batchilder**, College of the North Atlantic, Qatar; **Nicole Cuddie**, Community College of Qatar, Qatar; **Mahdi Duris**, King Saud University, Saudi Arabia; **Ahmed Ege**, Institute of Public Administration, Saudi Arabia; **Magda Fadle**, Victoria College, Egypt; **Mohammed Hassan**, Taibah University, Saudi Arabia; **Tom Hodgson**, Community College of Qatar, Qatar; **Ayub Agbar Khan**, Taibah University, Saudi Arabia; **Cynthia Le Joncour**, Taibah University, Saudi Arabia; **Ruari Alexander MacLeod**, Community College of Qatar, Qatar; **Nasir Mahmood**, Taibah University, Saudi Arabia; **Duria Salih Mahmoud**, Taibah University, Saudi Arabia; **Ameera McKoy**, Taibah University, Saudi Arabia; **Chaker Mhamdi**, Buraimi University College, Oman; **Baraa Shiekh Mohamed**, Community College of Qatar, Qatar; **Abduleelah Mohammed**, Taibah University, Saudi Arabia; **Shumaila Nasir**, Taibah University, Saudi Arabia; **Kevin Onwordi**, Taibah University, Saudi Arabia; **Dr. Navid Rahmani**, Community College of Qatar, Qatar; **Dr. Sabah Salman Sabbah**, Community College of Qatar, Qatar; **Salih**, Taibah University, Saudi Arabia; **Verna Santos-Nafrada**, King Saud University, Saudi Arabia; **Gamal Abdelfattah Shehata**, Taibah University, Saudi Arabia; **Ron Stefan**, Institute of Public Administration, Saudi Arabia; **Dr. Saad Torki**, Imam Abdulrahman Bin Faisal University, Dammam, Saudi Arabia; **Silvia Yafai**, Applied Technology High School/Secondary Technical School, UAE; **Mahmood Zar**, Taibah University, Saudi Arabia; **Thouraya Zheni**, Taibah University, Saudi Arabia

Turkey

Sema Babacan, Istanbul Medipol University; **Bilge Çöllüoğlu Yakar**, Bilkent University; **Liana Corniel**, Koc University; **Savas Geylanioglu**, Izmir Bahcesehir Science and Technology College; **Öznur Güler**, Giresun University; **Selen Bilginer Halefoğlu**, Maltepe University; **Ahmet Konukoğlu**, Hasan Kalyoncu University; **Mehmet Salih Yoğun**, Gaziantep Hasan Kalyoncu University; **Fatih Yücel**, Beykent University

Europe

Amina Al Hashamia, University of Exeter, UK; **Irina Gerasimova**, Saint-Petersburg Mining University, Russia; **Jodi**, Las Dominicas, Spain; **Marina Khanykova**, School 179, Russia; **Oksana Postnikova**, Lingua Practica, Russia; **Nina Vasilchenko**, Soho-Bridge Language School, Russia

CRITICAL THINKING

The unique critical thinking approach of the *Q: Skills for Success* series has been further enhanced in the Third Edition. New features help you analyze, synthesize, and develop your ideas.

Unit question

The thought-provoking unit questions engage you with the topic and provide a critical thinking framework for the unit.

UNIT QUESTION

How do you make a good first impression?

A. Discuss these questions with your classmates.

1. What qualities do you look for in a friend?

2. What is the best way to make a good first impression on a classmate? On a boss?

3. Look at the photo. Describe the people in the room. Where are they? What is the man standing up doing?

B. Listen to *The Q Classroom* online. Then complete the chart with the suggestions from the box.

Analysis

You can discuss your opinion of each reading text and analyze how it changes your perspective on the unit question.

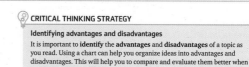

G. **DISCUSS** Work with a partner. Make a list of decisions you made today. Which ones do you think were lazy? Which ones were not lazy?

iQ PRACTICE Go online for additional reading and comprehension. *Practice > Unit 6 > Activity 4*

WRITE WHAT YOU THINK

A. **DISCUSS** Discuss the questions in a group. Think about the Unit Question, "Are you a good decision maker?"

1. Do you think you are a lazy thinker when you make decisions? Why or why not?

2. When did you make a decision using hard thinking? Was it a good decision?

3. When you meet someone new, can you tell if the person is honest or not? How?

B. **COMPOSE** Choose one of the questions from Activity A and write a paragraph in response. Look back at your Quick Write on page 132 as you think about what you learned.

NEW! Critical Thinking Strategy with video

Each unit includes a Critical Thinking Strategy with activities to give you step-by-step guidance in critical analysis of texts. An accompanying instructional video (available on iQ Online) provides extra support and examples.

CRITICAL THINKING STRATEGY

Identifying advantages and disadvantages

It is important to **identify** the **advantages** and **disadvantages** of a topic as you read. Using a chart can help you organize ideas into advantages and disadvantages. This will help you to compare and evaluate them better when writing and help you make a more informed opinion about the topic.

iQ PRACTICE Go online to watch the Critical Thinking Video and check your comprehension. *Practice > Unit 3 > Activity 4*

G. **CATEGORIZE** Complete the graphic organizer using your own words. Identify the advantages and disadvantages of driverless cars. Write the paragraph number where the answer is found.

Advantages of driverless cars	Disadvantages of driverless cars
• They can help people stay safe.	• They can't anticipate unexpected things like people can.
Paragraph: _4_	Paragraph: _5_
• _____	• _____
Paragraph: ____	Paragraph: ____
• _____	• _____
Paragraph: ____	Paragraph: ____
• _____	• _____
Paragraph: ____	Paragraph: ____

NEW! Bloom's Taxonomy

Blue activity headings integrate verbs from Bloom's Taxonomy to help you see how each activity develops critical thinking skills.

H. **DISCUSS** Work with a partner. Discuss how the advantages and disadvantages of driverless cars would affect transportation in the future.

iQ PRACTICE Go online for additional reading and comprehension. *Practice > Unit 3 > Activity 5*

THREE TYPES OF VIDEO

UNIT VIDEO

The unit videos include high-interest documentaries and reports on a wide variety of subjects, all linked to the unit topic and question.

NEW! "Work with the Video" pages guide you in watching, understanding, and discussing the unit videos. The activities help you see the connection to the Unit Question and the other texts in the unit.

CRITICAL THINKING VIDEO

NEW! Narrated by the Q series authors, these short videos give you further instruction into the Critical Thinking Strategy of each unit using engaging images and graphics. You can use them to get a deeper understanding of the Critical Thinking Strategy.

SKILLS VIDEO

NEW! These instructional videos provide illustrated explanations of skills and grammar points in the Student Book. They can be viewed in class or assigned for a flipped classroom, for homework, or for review. One skill video is available for every unit.

Easily access all videos in the Resources section of iQ Online.

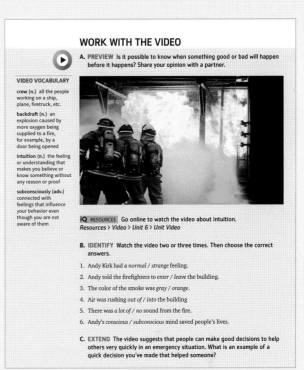

WORK WITH THE VIDEO

A. PREVIEW Is it possible to know when something good or bad will happen before it happens? Share your opinion with a partner.

VIDEO VOCABULARY

crew (n.) all the people working on a ship, plane, firetruck, etc.

backdraft (n.) an explosion caused by more oxygen being supplied to a fire, for example, by a door being opened

intuition (n.) the feeling or understanding that makes you believe or know something without any reason or proof

subconsciously (adv.) connected with feelings that influence your behavior even though you are not aware of them

iQ RESOURCES Go online to watch the video about intuition.
Resources > Video > Unit 6 > Unit Video

B. IDENTIFY Watch the video two or three times. Then choose the correct answers.

1. Andy Kirk had a *normal / strange* feeling.
2. Andy told the firefighters to *enter / leave* the building.
3. The color of the smoke was *gray / orange*.
4. Air was rushing *out of / into* the building.
5. There was *a lot of / no* sound from the fire.
6. Andy's *conscious / subconscious* mind saved people's lives.

C. EXTEND The video suggests that people can make good decisions to help others very quickly in an emergency situation. What is an example of a quick decision you've made that helped someone?

How to compare and contrast

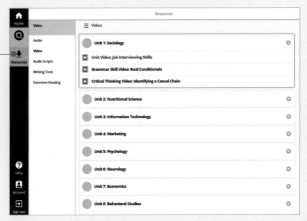

VOCABULARY

A research-based vocabulary program focuses on the words you need to know academically and professionally.

The vocabulary syllabus in *Q: Skills for Success* is correlated to the CEFR (see page 212) and linked to two word lists: the Oxford 3000 and the OPAL (Oxford Phrasal Academic Lexicon).

⚘ OXFORD 3000

The Oxford 3000 lists the core words that every learner at the A1– B2 level needs to know. Items in the word list are selected for their frequency and usefulness from the Oxford English Corpus (a database of over 2 billion words).

Vocabulary Key
In vocabulary activities, ⚘ shows you the word is in the Oxford 3000 and **OPAL** shows you the word or phrase is in the OPAL.

☐ to explain the sport of Formula 1 car racing

☐ to encourage businesses to invest in car racing

☐ to compare Formula 1 car races around the world

☐ to show why car racing is an expensive sport

B. QUICK WRITE What are some ways businesses attract more customers? Write for 5–10 minutes in response. Be sure to use this section for your Unit Assignment.

C. VOCABULARY Check (✓) the words you know. Then work with a partner to locate each word in the reading. Use clues to help define the words you don't know. Check your definitions in the dictionary.

assured *(adj.)*	invest *(v.)* ⚘	profit *(n.)* ⚘
dependable *(adj.)*	logo *(n.)*	sponsor *(v.)* ⚘
expansion *(n.)* OPAL	market *(n.)* ⚘	stability *(n.)* OPAL
image *(n.)* ⚘ OPAL		

⚘ Oxford 3000™ words   **OPAL** Oxford Phrasal Academic Lexicon

iQ PRACTICE Go online to listen and practice your pronunciation.
Practice > Unit 8 > Activity 2

OPAL
OXFORD PHRASAL ACADEMIC LEXICON

NEW! The OPAL is a collection of four word lists that provide an essential guide to the most important words and phrases to know for academic English. The word lists are based on the Oxford Corpus of Academic English and the British Academic Spoken English corpus. The OPAL includes both spoken and written academic English and both individual words and longer phrases.

Academic Language tips in the Student Book give information about how words and phrases from the OPAL are used and offer help with features such as collocations and phrasal verbs.

ACADEMIC LANGUAGE
The corpus shows that
based on is often used
in academic writing.
Based on the results . . .
. . . the research
was based on . . .

──────────── OPAL
Oxford Phrasal Academic Lexicon

3. Jack's question at the meeting was not _____ of low sales; it was completely off topic.

4. Sam recommended some articles on the effects of online a These articles _____ his own views, based has done.

5. Mr. Santana needs to _____ that marketing profession for him. He needs to find another area that will skills better.

6. If you plan to study in a financial area such as accounting, sure that your work is always _____.

7. One _____ that has caused changes in adv popularity of social media.

8. People are constantly on their smartphones; this has had a _____ on how people communicate.

9. The students are looking at their phones. This _____ instructor that they are not interested in the class.

iQ PRACTICE Go online for more practice with the vocabul
Practice > Unit 4 > Activity 3

C. IDENTIFY Read the main ideas. Write the paragraph nu are found.

EXTENSIVE READING

NEW! Extensive Reading is a program of reading for pleasure at a level that matches your language ability.

There are many benefits to Extensive Reading:

- It helps you to become a better reader in general.
- It helps to increase your reading speed.
- It can improve your reading comprehension.
- It increases your vocabulary range.
- It can improve your grammar and writing skills.
- It's great for motivation—reading something that is interesting for its own sake.

Each unit of *Q: Skills for Success* Third Edition has been aligned to an Oxford Graded Reader based on the appropriate topic and level of language proficiency. The first chapter of each recommended graded reader can be downloaded from iQ Online Resources.

iQ ONLINE extends your learning beyond the classroom.

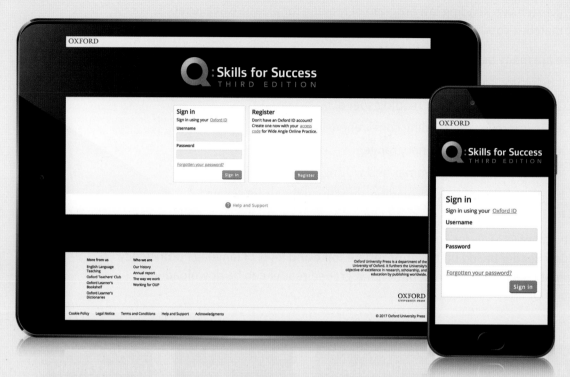

- Practice activities provide essential skills practice and support.
- Automatic grading and progress reports show you what you have mastered and where you still need more practice.
- Discussion Board to discuss the Unit Questions helps you develop your critical thinking.
- Writing Tutor helps you practice your academic writing skills.
- Essential resources such as audio and video are easy to access anytime.

NEW TO THE THIRD EDITION

- Site is optimized for mobile use so you can use it on your phone.
- An updated interface allows easy navigation around the activities, tests, resources, and scores.
- New Critical Thinking Videos expand on the Critical Thinking Strategies in the Student Book.
- Extensive Reading program helps you improve your vocabulary and reading skills.

How to use
iQ ONLINE

Go to **Practice** to find additional practice and support to complement your learning in the classroom.

Go to **Resources** to find
- All Student Book video
- All Student Book audio
- Critical Thinking videos
- Skills videos
- Extensive Reading

Go to **Messages** and **Discussion Board** to communicate with your teacher and classmates.

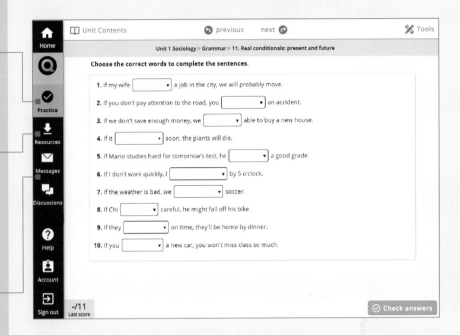

Online tests assigned by your teacher help you assess your progress and see where you still need more practice.

Progress bar shows you how many activities you have completed.

View your scores for all activities.

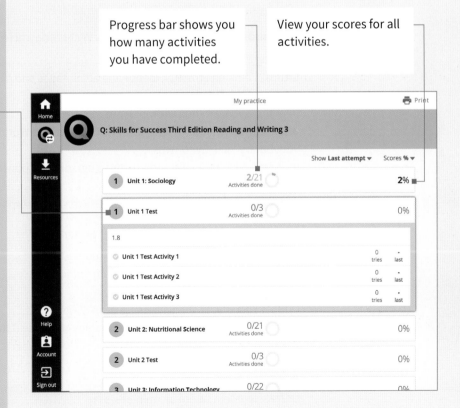

CONTENTS

Sociology

UNIT QUESTION

How do you make a good first impression?

A. Discuss these questions with your classmates.

1. What qualities do you look for in a friend?

2. What is the best way to make a good first impression on a classmate? On a boss?

3. Look at the photo. Describe the people in the room. Where are they? What is the man standing up doing?

B. Listen to *The Q Classroom* online. Then complete the chart with the suggestions from the box.

be polite	~~comb my hair~~	have confidence
keep eye contact	pay attention	remember people's
smile	~~wear nice clothes~~	names

How do you make a good first impression?	
Marcus	comb my hair, wear nice clothes
Yuna	
Felix	
Sophy	

iQ PRACTICE Go to the online discussion board to discuss the Unit Question with your classmates. *Practice > Unit 1 > Activity 1*

UNIT OBJECTIVE

Read the articles and gather information and ideas to write a paragraph on how to make a good first impression.

3

READING 1

OBJECTIVE ▶

Small Talk: A Big Deal

You are going to read a newspaper article about small talk. Use the article to gather information and ideas for your Unit Assignment.

PREVIEW THE READING

A. PREVIEW Read the title and headings and look at the photographs. What do you think "small talk" means? Check (✓) your answer.

☐ talking about important events in your life

☐ talking about things like traffic or weather

☐ talking about your boss and coworkers

WRITING TIP

When you do your Quick Write, try to keep writing without stopping. Focus on your ideas.

B. QUICK WRITE How do you feel when you meet someone new at school or at work? What do you say to make him or her feel more comfortable? Write for 5–10 minutes in response. Be sure to use this section for your Unit Assignment.

C. VOCABULARY Check (✓) the words you know. Then work with a partner to locate each word in the reading. Use clues to help define the words you don't know. Check your definitions in the dictionary.

appreciate *(v.)* 🔑	impress *(v.)* 🔑	offensive *(adj.)* 🔑
confidence *(n.)* 🔑	lead to *(v. phr.)*	select *(v.)* 🔑 OPAL
demonstrate *(v.)* 🔑 OPAL	maintain *(v.)* 🔑 OPAL	stranger *(n.)* 🔑
effective *(adj.)* 🔑 OPAL		

🔑 Oxford 3000™ words   **OPAL** Oxford Phrasal Academic Lexicon

iQ PRACTICE Go online to listen and practice your pronunciation.
Practice › Unit 1 › Activity 2

WORK WITH THE READING

 A. INVESTIGATE Read the article and gather information about how to make a good first impression.

SMALL TALK: A BIG DEAL

1   Put a group of **strangers** in a room together, and they'll probably start a conversation. "Hot today, isn't it?" one might say. "You said it," another replies. Soon enough, comments about today's weather will **lead to** other people's weather stories about getting stuck in the rain or trying to stay cool during last week's high of 100 degrees Fahrenheit (37.7 degrees Celsius).

2   Why do we talk so much about the weather, and why is it important? When we first meet people, we don't begin by telling them our life story. We start with *small talk*, a polite conversation about something much less important, like traffic or weather. Sometimes it goes nowhere. We may talk to people in the elevator, at the store, or on the bus, but the conversation quickly ends. Many other times, however, small talk can create something *much* bigger, including new friendships or even a better job. It just has to be done the right way.

New Friends and Jobs

3   Research suggests that small talk can build new friendships. When we begin conversations with new people, we want to feel comfortable, and so do they. We use small talk to find common interests. Weather may lead to more interesting topics like summer fashion or winter foods. Once we have a common interest, a friendship can begin. The more we engage in[1] small talk, the more friends we can make.

4   Small talk even helps people get hired and perform better at work. In order to **impress** at a job interview, you need to bond with the interviewer right away. **Effective** small talk can make that first impression get you the job. Small talk is equally important after you are hired. In fact, research **demonstrates** that just five minutes of small talk can lead to more successful business deals. Effective small talk at the office can also help people get promoted[2] more often.

[1] **engage in:** to take part in something
[2] **promote:** to move someone to a higher rank or more senior job

As Easy as 1–2–3

5   So, how can you make small talk lead to a new friendship, job, or promotion? First off, find common ground. **Select** something around you that you share with the other person. At a job interview, look around the room for common interests. Perhaps the interviewer has a photo of his children on his desk. "Oh, you have kids, too?" you might ask.

6   Next, keep the conversation going. Compliment[3] the other person to make him or her feel comfortable and ask questions to show interest: "Oh, you've been to Paris?" Don't do all the talking and avoid saying anything **offensive** that might make the other person feel awkward. It could create a negative impression and possibly end the conversation.

7   Third, **maintain** eye contact. When you look people in the eye, they feel you **appreciate** what they are saying. Maintaining eye contact is important. It makes you appear honest and builds trust. Without trust, a relationship cannot develop[4], say experts.

The Big Question: To Talk or Not to Talk?

8   Some people shy away from small talk. They might not have enough **confidence** to start up conversations with strangers. And let's face it—talking to someone you don't know is not the easiest thing to do! Still, experts say with practice, small talk *does* get easier, even for the shy ones. You just have to take that first step.

9   Other people avoid small talk because they dislike discussing things like traffic, weather, or sports scores. For them, these topics are just *too* small. However, when you think about it, small talk is anything but small. In fact, it is actually a *very* big deal!

[3] **compliment:** to praise or express admiration for someone
[4] **develop:** to become better and stronger

B. VOCABULARY Here are some words from Reading 1. Read the sentences. Then match each bold word with its definition below.

_f_ 1. I thought I saw a **stranger** standing in front of my apartment building, but then I realized it was my friend waiting for me.

_i_ 2. Smiling can **demonstrate** to other people that you are a friendly person. Shaking a person's hand is another way to show friendliness.

_b_ 3. People with **confidence** usually make better public speakers because they feel very comfortable standing in front of a lot of people.

_d_ 4. Many people believe Facebook is an **effective** way to keep in touch with family and friends who live far away.

_a_ 5. When you meet new people in school, it can sometimes **lead to** friendships that last a lifetime.

_e_ 6. You should **select** what you wear to a job interview carefully. What you wear to an interview is very important.

_g_ 7. I really **appreciate** my friends. They always give me good advice.

_c_ 8. Adel wanted to **impress** the interviewer, so he told him about the important project he worked on.

_j_ 9. One of the best ways to **maintain** a conversation is to keep asking questions; then it can easily continue.

_h_ 10. Jokes are a great way to "break the ice" when you meet new people, but you should never tell **offensive** jokes that could make them feel uncomfortable or angry.

a. *(v. phr.)* to have something as a result

b. *(n.)* the feeling that you are sure about your own beliefs or abilities

c. *(v.)* to make someone admire and respect you

d. *(adj.)* producing the result that is wanted or intended

e. *(v.)* to choose someone or something from similar people or things

f. *(n.)* a person you do not know

g. *(v.)* to enjoy or to understand the value of someone or something

h. *(adj.)* unpleasant or insulting

i. *(v.)* to show clearly that something exists or is true

j. *(v.)* to continue to have something; to keep something at the same level

iQ PRACTICE Go online for more practice with the vocabulary.
Practice › Unit 1 › Activity 3

C. RESTATE Circle the main idea of the article.

a. Strangers who find themselves together in the same place will probably talk to each other.

b. Small talk is a polite conversation with strangers about topics like traffic, weather, or sports.

c. According to experts, there are three important steps to follow when you engage in small talk.

d. When small talk is done correctly, it can improve people's social and professional lives.

D. CATEGORIZE Read the statements. Write *T* (true) or *F* (false). Then correct each false statement to make it true according to the article.

_____ 1. People do not usually talk about their personal lives with strangers.

_____ 2. Small talk can happen at the store or on the bus.

_____ 3. Small talk helps people find shared interests.

_____ 4. Small talk is only helpful before you get a job.

_____ 5. Just five minutes of small talk helps employees get promoted.

_____ 6. You should never ask new people details about their family.

_____ 7. Some people feel uncomfortable using small talk.

_____ 8. Effective small talk can leave a bad first impression on others.

TIP FOR SUCCESS

Use pronoun referents, such as *it* and *they*, to continue an idea in a following sentence.

E. IDENTIFY Read these sentences from Reading 1. Then answer the questions. Find the sentences in the reading to help you.

1. (Paragraph 1) Put a group of strangers in a room together, and **they**'ll probably start a conversation.

   Who does *they* refer to? _____

2. (Paragraph 2) **It** just has to be done the right way.

   What does *it* refer to? _____

3. (Paragraph 3) When we begin conversations with new people, we want to feel comfortable, and so do **they**.

   Who does *they* refer to? _____

4. (Paragraph 6) **It** could create a negative impression and possibly end the conversation.

   What does *it* refer to? _____

5. (Paragraph 7) **It** makes you appear honest and builds trust.

   What does *it* refer to? _____

6. (Paragraph 8) **They** might not have enough confidence to start up conversations with strangers.

   Who does *they* refer to? _____

 ## CRITICAL THINKING STRATEGY

Identifying a causal chain

A **causal chain** is a series of causes and effects. When you organize ideas into a causal chain, it will help you to see how one event affects another event, which then affects another event.

Be careful not to confuse a list of chronological (time) events with a series of causes and events. Time order is a different relationship from a cause-effect relationship.

iQ PRACTICE Go online to watch the Critical Thinking Video and check your comprehension. *Practice > Unit 1 > Activity 4*

F. IDENTIFY Read paragraph 3 of Reading 1 and complete this graphic organizer. Identify the causal chain in the paragraph. Write the correct answers in the boxes.

b →   →   →   →

a. We find common interests.

b. We begin a conversation with a stranger.

c. A new friendship starts.

d. We discuss more interesting topics.

e. We use small talk.

G. COMPOSE The author suggests that there is also a *wrong* way to use small talk. What do you think the wrong way might be? Write a paragraph of 5–8 sentences giving your opinion. Then share your paragraph with a partner and compare your ideas.

iQ PRACTICE Go online for additional reading and comprehension. *Practice > Unit 1 > Activity 5*

WRITE WHAT YOU THINK

A. DISCUSS Discuss the questions in a group.

1. When was the last time you used small talk? Describe the situation.

2. Do you agree with the author that small talk is "a big deal"? Why or why not?

B. COMPOSE Choose one question and write a paragraph in response. Look back at your Quick Write on page 4 as you think about what you learned.

READING SKILL Identifying main ideas and supporting details

A paragraph is a group of sentences about the same topic. The **main idea** is usually given in the first sentence. This is called the *topic sentence*. Sometimes the topic sentence can also be the last sentence or in the middle of a paragraph. The other sentences are called *supporting sentences* and contain **supporting details**, such as examples, explanations, facts, definitions, and reasons.

Identifying main ideas and supporting details is an important skill that will help you become a more effective reader. When you read, skim for main ideas and scan for details.

A. CATEGORIZE Read these sentences from Reading 1. Write *MI* for the main idea of the paragraph. Write *SD* for the supporting details.

1. Paragraph 3

    ＿＿ a. Weather may lead to a more interesting topic like summer fashion or winter foods.

    ＿＿ b. Research suggests that small talk can build new friendships.

    ＿＿ c. The more we engage in small talk, the more friends we can make.

2. Paragraph 4

    ＿＿ a. In order to impress at a job interview, you need to bond with the interviewer right away.

    ＿＿ b. In fact, research demonstrates that just five minutes of small talk can lead to more successful business deals.

    ＿＿ c. Small talk even helps people get hired and perform better at work.

3. Paragraph 5

    ＿＿ a. So, how can you make small talk lead to a new friendship, job, or promotion?

    ＿＿ b. First off, find common ground.

    ＿＿ c. At a job interview, look around the room for common interests.

B. IDENTIFY Look again at paragraphs 1, 6, 7, and 8 in Reading 1. Underline the topic sentence that states each paragraph's main idea. Then compare your answers with a partner.

iQ PRACTICE Go online for more practice identifying main ideas and supporting details. *Practice > Unit 1 > Activity 6*

READING 2

OBJECTIVE ▶

21st Century Job Interviews

You are going to read an interview with a career counselor about job interviews. Use the article to gather information and ideas for your Unit Assignment.

PREVIEW THE READING

A. PREVIEW Read the title and the questions the interviewer asks. Check (✓) all the topics you expect the interview to cover.

- ☐ how the Internet has affected job interviewing
- ☐ why employers use social media
- ☐ how to find jobs through other people
- ☐ how to make a video interview
- ☐ what the perfect résumé looks like

ACADEMIC LANGUAGE
The corpus shows that *expect* and *responsible* are more common in academic writing than academic speaking.

──────────── **OPAL**
Oxford Phrasal Academic Lexicon

B. QUICK WRITE What advice would you give to someone on a job interview? What should he or she do and not do? Write for 5–10 minutes in response. Be sure to use this section for your Unit Assignment.

C. VOCABULARY Check (✓) the words you know. Use a dictionary to define any new or unknown words. Then discuss how the words will relate to the unit with a partner.

accomplishment *(n.)*	professional *(adj.)* 🔑 OPAL	slang *(n.)*
authentic *(adj.)*	punctual *(adj.)*	weakness *(n.)* 🔑
consider *(v.)* 🔑 OPAL	research *(n.)* 🔑 OPAL	
expect *(v.)* 🔑 OPAL	responsible *(adj.)* 🔑 OPAL	

🔑 Oxford 3000™ words   **OPAL** Oxford Phrasal Academic Lexicon

iQ PRACTICE Go online to listen and practice your pronunciation.
Practice > Unit 1 > Activity 7

WORK WITH THE READING

 A. INVESTIGATE Read the interview and gather information about how to make a good first impression.

21ˢᵀ CENTURY JOB INTERVIEWS

Rose Dubois is a career counselor in Paris, France. She has spent the last 20 years helping people prepare for the job of their dreams. Dubois notes that job interviewing in the 21ˢᵗ century is a very different game than it was before. It's not about the perfect résumé anymore. With so much information on the Internet, people have to be even more prepared and more careful if they expect to get the perfect job. CareersToday.com sat down with Dubois in a little cafe in the south of Paris, and here's what she had to say.

CareersToday: So, why is job interviewing so different in the 21ˢᵗ century?

Dubois: Well, a lot of it has to do with social media. Over 90 percent of interviewers look at people's social media pages. And they don't just look at **professional** sites like LinkedIn. They also go to their personal pages on Facebook and read their tweets on Twitter.

CareersToday: And do you **consider** social media a bad thing?

Dubois: Well, it just means that you have to be careful about what you put on there. For one, use your real name. Don't use a nickname or another funny name that your friends have given you. Employers want to know it's you. Also, make sure you use the same profile picture everywhere. Employers need to know it's the same person.

CareersToday: Are there any other ways job interviews have changed because of the Internet?

Dubois: Oh, definitely. The most successful candidates do **research** online before the interview. They visit the company's website to find out more about the company. For example, what's the name of the president or CEO? What's the company's history? What are its goals for the future? If you know the answers to these questions, they'll know you're taking the position seriously, and you'll be more successful.

CareersToday: Those are all great points. However, isn't it also true that a lot of interviews aren't even in person anymore?

Dubois: Yes, absolutely. To save money, more and more employers are asking people for video interviews. So, they'll email you a list of questions, and then you have to record your answers on camera and send the video back to them. Unfortunately, not everyone is a YouTube star, so there are certain tips to keep in mind.

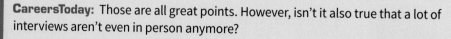

CareersToday: Great. What are those tips?

Dubois: Well, first off, dress professionally. Wearing business clothes, like a nice suit, is a great way to impress. Don't just wear a T-shirt and jeans! And two, watch how you talk. If you talk too fast, they won't understand you. If you're too slow, they'll get bored. You should also avoid using any **slang** or bad words. They won't impress anybody!

CareersToday: And how can people prepare to make the video?

Dubois: Practice, practice, practice. Practice your answers off camera lots of times before you put them on camera. You can write them down so you know what to say, but don't read them when you make the video. You want to look as natural as possible, and if you read them, it won't look **authentic**. And when you do record the video, make sure there's enough light. It makes a bad impression when the interviewer can't even see your face.

CareersToday: Well, a lot really has changed in the 21st century. Is there anything that hasn't changed? That's still the same?

Dubois: Oh, sure. During the interview, don't be afraid to sell yourself. Talk about your **accomplishments**. Employers still want people who are confident in their abilities. But also, be honest about your **weaknesses**. If you are doing a video recording, don't look down or look away a lot. You want to appear focused and present. And if the interview is in person[1], make sure to keep eye contact the whole time. Keeping eye contact always shows that you are both honest and confident.

CareersToday: Great. Any last advice?

Dubois: Yes, two things. First, be **punctual**. Don't miss the deadline for your video interview, and don't arrive late to in-person interviews. No employer wants to hire someone who is not **responsible** enough to come to work on time. Get there 10–15 minutes early to help yourself relax.

CareersToday: And the second one?

Dubois: Don't forget to smile!

[1] **in person:** with the personal presence or action of the person mentioned

B. VOCABULARY Complete each sentence with the vocabulary from Reading 2.

10 accomplishment (n.)   9 professional (adj.)   6 responsible (adj.)

محبوب- اصیل 1 authentic (adj.)   4 punctual (adj.)   5 slang (n.)

3 consider (v.)   8 research (n.)   2 weakness (n.)

7 expect (v.)

1. The job interviewer didn't think that Scott was very _____. He didn't keep eye contact, and his answers didn't seem natural or honest.

2. My boss is a great person, but he has one _____. He almost never smiles, even when things are going well!

3. You are not allowed to use your cell phone in some restaurants because many people _____ it rude.

4. Alain is always _____. He's never late for anything.

5. Many teenagers use so much _____ when they talk to each other that their own parents can't understand them.

6. Takeshi is very _____. He always pays his bills on time.

7. You were late for work again today. I _____ you to arrive on time tomorrow.

8. A friend told me about a good company, so I did some _____ online. I learned that it was one of the top companies to work for here.

9. When you speak to customers, you should always be _____. You should be polite and try to help them as quickly as you can.

10. Getting a job as an accountant has been my greatest professional _____. It's something I dreamed about for years.

iQ PRACTICE Go online for more practice with the vocabulary.
Practice > Unit 1 > Activity 8

C. IDENTIFY Complete the T-chart with information from the article.

Job interviewing *dos*	Job interviewing *don'ts*
Be careful on social media.	Don't use a nickname on social media.

D. CATEGORIZE Read the statements. Write *T* (true) or *F* (false). Then correct each false statement to make it true according to the article.

____ 1. Learn as much as you can about the company before the interview.

____ 2. Most companies expect you to wear casual clothes in a video interview.

____ 3. Arrive 30–40 minutes early so you can start the interview early.

____ 4. Keeping eye contact shows that you are confident.

____ 5. It's OK if your name on social media is different from your real name.

____ 6. Be honest when talking about your weaknesses.

____ 7. It's better to talk very slowly during a job interview.

E. INVESTIGATE Match these main ideas from the reading with the correct supporting details below. Then read the article again to check your answers.

____ 1. Be careful online.

____ 2. Do research online.

____ 3. Dress professionally.

____ 4. Watch how you talk.

____ 5. Be prepared for a video-recorded interview.

____ 6. Sell yourself.

____ 7. Keep eye contact.

____ 8. Be punctual.

a. Practice your answers off camera before you make the recording.

b. Show the interviewer that you are honest and confident.

c. Find out about the company's history, culture, and goals on its website.

d. Use the same profile picture on Facebook, LinkedIn, and other social media websites.

e. Wearing business clothes, like a nice suit, is a great way to impress.

f. Remember not to use any slang or bad words.

g. Don't be afraid to talk about your accomplishments.

h. No employer wants to hire someone who is not responsible enough to come to work on time.

WORK WITH THE VIDEO

A. PREVIEW How do you feel when you walk into a job interview? Why? Discuss your ideas with a partner.

VIDEO VOCABULARY

generic (adj.) describing a general type of something, not one thing in particular

rattle through (v. phr.) to say something very quickly

common ground (n.) opinions or interests shared by two or more people

scale (v.) to observe

iQ RESOURCES Go online to watch the video about job interviewing skills.
Resources > Video > Unit 1 > Unit Video

B. IDENTIFY Watch the first two and a half minutes of the video two or three times. Then circle the answers.

1. You *can / can't* change a first impression.

2. If someone offers you water at a meeting, say *yes / no*.

3. Most people think they only need to *answer / prepare* interview questions.

4. It's best to ask *generic / specific* questions at a job interview.

5. You should position yourself as an *insider / outsider* of the company.

6. Look for common ground *before / after* the meeting.

C. EXTEND What are other mistakes people can make at job interviews? Discuss your ideas with a partner.

WRITE WHAT YOU THINK

SYNTHESIZE Think about Reading 1, Reading 2, and the unit video as you discuss these questions. Then choose one question and write a paragraph in response.

1. What are the best ways to make a good impression on others?

2. Can you make a good first impression the same way in every situation (at a job interview, talking to a customer, meeting a new classmate, etc.)? Why or why not?

VOCABULARY SKILL Using the dictionary to identify word forms

Learning **word forms** increases your vocabulary. It will help make your reading, speaking, and writing more fluent. Look at the dictionary definitions below.

> **ac·com·plish** /ə'kɑmplɪʃ/ *verb* [T] to succeed in doing something difficult that you planned to do: *Very little was accomplished at the meeting.* **SYN** achieve

> **ac·com·plished** /ə'kɑmplɪʃt/ *adj.* highly skilled at something: *an accomplished pianist*

> **ac·com·plish·ment** /ə'kɑmplɪʃmənt/ *noun* **1** [C] something difficult that someone has succeeded in doing or learning: *He was proud of his academic accomplishments.* **2** *(formal)* [U] the act of completing something successfully

All dictionary entries adapted from the *Oxford American Dictionary for learners of English* © Oxford University Press 2011.

A. IDENTIFY Complete the chart. An *X* indicates that a word form doesn't exist or you don't need to know it at this time. Use your dictionary to help you.

TIP FOR SUCCESS

Many words have the same noun and verb form. For example, *tie* can be a noun or a verb.

Noun	Verb	Adjective	Adverb
1. accomplishment	accomplish	accomplished	X
2. confidence	X	confident, confidential	confidentially
3. consideration	consider	considerable	considerably
4. demonstration	demonstrate	demonstrative	X
5. impression	impress	impressive	impressively
6. offense	offend	offensive	offensively
7. responsibility	X	responsible	responsibly
8. selection	select	selective	selectively

B. APPLY Complete each sentence with a word from the chart in Activity A.

1. My biggest ___accomplishment___ in life so far has been my graduation from high school.

2. Appearance is an important ___consideration___ if you want to make a good impression. Think carefully about how you will look to others.

3. When you speak in public, you need to show ___confidence___.
Even if you are nervous, you should look as if you are not.

4. Keeping eye contact will ___demonstrate___ to others that you are interested in what they are saying.

5. The person who applied for the job had a(n) ___impressive___ work history. The manager was surprised at the high-level positions she had held.

6. Don't tell jokes when you meet people for the first time because you might ___offend___ them and make them angry or upset.

C. COMPOSE Choose two sets of words from Activity A. Write one sentence for each form of the word. Then share your sentences with a partner.

iQ PRACTICE Go online for more practice using the dictionary to identify word forms. *Practice > Unit 1 > Activity 9*

WRITING

OBJECTIVE ▶ At the end of this unit, you will write a paragraph about how to make a good first impression. This paragraph will include specific information from the readings, the unit video, and your own ideas.

WRITING SKILL Part 1 Organizing and developing a paragraph

A paragraph should discuss one main idea from beginning to end and develop the main idea with specific details.

- The **topic sentence** is usually the first sentence of a paragraph. It identifies the topic, or subject, of the paragraph. It also gives the main idea (or controlling idea), which explains what the writer will say about the topic.

- The **supporting sentences** are the middle sentences of a paragraph. They support the topic sentence with two or three smaller ideas, or subtopics. Subtopics are supported with specific details, such as examples, explanations, facts, definitions, and reasons.

- The **concluding sentence** is usually the last sentence of a paragraph. It summarizes the main points of the paragraph and restates the topic sentence, but in different words.

A. WRITING MODEL Read the model paragraph. Then answer the questions.

1. What is the topic sentence of the paragraph? Circle it.

How to Annoy Your Coworkers

When you start a job, you can leave a bad impression on your new coworkers very quickly without even realizing it. Because the workplace can be fast-paced and stressful, it can be easy to forget the people around you. One sure way to annoy your coworkers is to speak loudly on your phone. This can make it difficult for your coworkers to focus on what they are doing or to have phone conversations of their own. It may also send a message that you think your work and phone conversations are more important than anyone else's. Another common mistake is to take the last cup of coffee and not make another pot. This means that the next person has to make a new pot. Nobody likes to do this, particularly first thing in the morning! Many people find this behavior very rude. Leaving your cell phone on is another way you could unknowingly irritate your coworkers. Your ringing cell phone may disturb the quiet your coworkers need to do their work. The noise may cause them to work more slowly or make mistakes. Also, many people consider it disrespectful. Finding your dream job may take a lot of time and effort, but unfortunately, leaving a bad impression on your coworkers can be done quickly and easily!

2. How many supporting sentences are in the paragraph? ____

3. The paragraph gives three ways to make a bad impression on your coworkers. What are these three subtopics? Write them below.

   a. _____

   b. _____

   c. _____

4. The paragraph uses reasons to support the subtopics. What reason explains why a ringing phone may cause people to make mistakes?

   _____

5. What is the concluding sentence of the paragraph? Underline it.

B. **ANALYZE** Complete the paragraph below. Choose the correct topic sentence and supporting details from the box. Use the information from Reading 1 to develop your ideas. One sentence will not be used.

   a. Find a shared interest or talk about what is around you, like your school or your teacher.
   b. Friends are easy to make at work.
   c. There are several ways to make new friends.
   d. For example, you could talk about your boss or your customers.

Making New Friends

____ First, if you go to school, you can make new friends in class. Come early
1
so you have time to meet other people before class starts, and try not to sit

by yourself. Instead, sit next to another student and use small talk to start

a conversation. ____ Soon you will discover what you have in common, and
2
your new friendship can develop! Another great place to make new friends is

at work. You and your coworkers will already have many things in common to

talk about. ____ If your friendship develops, you might even hang out, which
3
will give you something to look forward to after you finish work. Making new

friends is not always easy, but with a little effort, you can build friendships

with the people around you, and in the process, you may even find your new

best friend!

An **outline** is a plan you make before you start writing. Outlines help you put your ideas in order. When you write an outline for a paragraph, include the topic sentence, the subtopics, important supporting details, and the concluding sentence.

Example of an outline

1. **Topic sentence:** When you start a job, you can leave a bad impression on your new coworkers very quickly without even realizing it.

2. **Subtopics and supporting details:**
   A. talking loudly on your phone
      1. coworkers can't focus or have phone calls
      2. sends a message
   B. taking the last cup of coffee
      1. someone else has to make more
      2. many people find it rude
   C. leaving cell phone on
      1. coworkers may work more slowly or make mistakes
      2. many people consider it disrespectful

3. **Concluding sentence:** Finding your dream job may take a lot of time and effort, but unfortunately, leaving a bad impression on your coworkers can be done quickly and easily!

A. WRITING MODEL Read the model paragraph. Then complete the outline on page 22.

Fixing a Negative Impression

Sometimes we say something that leaves people with a bad impression, but it is possible to fix the situation. First, you must figure out why you have made others upset or uninterested. Think about the conversation you had earlier and try to remember what you said that offended others. For example, sometimes we tell a joke that they do not think is funny. Second, be prepared for the next time you see them. Make a plan about what you want to say and what topics you should avoid. You do not want to make the same mistake twice! Finally, when you see them again, be positive and act interested. Do not bring up the bad past experience. Instead, focus on the present. You should get them to talk a lot so that they feel more comfortable around you. Ask questions, listen carefully to their answers, and respond with thoughtful comments that show you care about what they have to say. There is no standard formula to turn a negative impression into a positive one; however, if you stay positive and seem interested in changing their opinion about you, you are more likely to get them to like you the next time!

1. Topic sentence: _Sometimes we say something that leaves people with a_
   bad impression, but it is possible to fix the situation.

2. Subtopics and supporting details:

   A. _____

      1. _Think about the conversation._

      2. _____

   B. _Be prepared._

      1. _____

      2. _____

   C. _____

      1. _Don't bring up the bad past experience._

      2. _____

3. Concluding sentence: _____

   _____

   _____

   _____

WRITING TIP
Use listing-order transition signals, such as *first*, *second*, and *third*, to introduce subtopics in a paragraph that gives steps or advice.

B. RESTATE Work with a partner or group to complete this outline for the paragraph in Activity B on page 20. Fill in the topic sentence, the remaining subtopic and supporting details, and a concluding sentence. Use your own ideas.

1. Topic sentence: _____

   _____

2. Subtopics and supporting details:

   A. _You can make new friends in class._

      1. _Come to class early._

      2. _____

      3. _____

   B. _____

      1. _____

      2. _____

3. Concluding sentence: _____

_____

_____

_____

iQ PRACTICE Go online for more practice with organizing and developing a paragraph. *Practice > Unit 1 > Activity 10*

GRAMMAR Real conditionals: present and future

The **present real conditional** is used to talk about general truths, habits, and things that happen again and again. It is formed by using the simple present in both the *if* clause (the condition) and the result clause.

> *if* clause   result clause
>
> If you **walk** in wearing jeans and a T-shirt, you **are not likely** to get the position.

You can also use a modal (*may, might, would, could*) in the result clause.

> *if* clause   result clause
>
> If you **disagree** too much in your first conversation, the other person **may think**
> you are hard to get along with.

The **future real conditional** is used to talk about what will happen under certain conditions. The *if* clause gives the condition. The result clause gives the result. The future real conditional is formed by using the simple present in the *if* clause and the future with *will* or *be going to* in the result clause.

> *if* clause   result clause
>
> If you **smile** frequently, it **will make** other people more comfortable.

> *if* clause   result clause
>
> If you **stay** honest and professional, you **will get** one step closer to the
> job you want.

You can also use *when* or *whenever* instead of *if* for both the present real conditional and the future real conditional.

> *when* clause   result clause
>
> When you **take care of** yourself, you **feel** better!

> result clause   *when* clause
>
> You**'ll impress** other people when you **practice** good listening skills.

iQ RESOURCES Go online to watch the Grammar Skill Video.
Resources > Video > Unit 1 > Grammar Skill Video

A. IDENTIFY Underline the *if* or *when* clause, and circle the result clause.

1. People want to be around you when you have good listening skills.
2. If you tell a joke, you could offend someone.
3. When you dress appropriately, people take you seriously.
4. You are more likely to make a good impression if you are confident and prepared.
5. If you don't ask questions, people may not think you're interested in what they're saying.

B. APPLY Complete each sentence with the correct form of the verb in parentheses. There may be more than one correct answer.

1. If they offer me the job, I think I _will take_ it. (take)
2. I _____ better when I exercise regularly. (feel)
3. If a student pays attention in class, the teacher _____ a good first impression of her or him. (have)
4. If you _____ unprepared, the interviewer might think you are not serious. (come)
5. He probably won't pass if he _____. (not, study)

C. Complete each sentence with your own ideas.

1. If you don't get enough sleep, _____.
2. If you don't prepare for the interview, _____.
3. If you don't pay attention to your friend, _____

_____.

4. If you tell a joke, _____.
5. If you arrive 15 minutes late to a job interview, _____

_____.

iQ PRACTICE Go online for more practice with real conditionals.
Practice > Unit 1 > Activities 11–12

UNIT ASSIGNMENT Write a "how to" paragraph

OBJECTIVE ▶

In this assignment, you are going to organize, develop, and write a "how to" paragraph. As you prepare your paragraph, think about the Unit Question, "How do you make a good first impression?" Use information from Reading 1, Reading 2, the unit video, and your work in this unit to support your "how to" paragraph. Refer to the Self-Assessment checklist on page 26.

iQ PRACTICE Go online to the Writing Tutor to read a model "how to" paragraph. *Practice > Unit 1 > Activity 13*

PLAN AND WRITE

A. BRAINSTORM Follow these steps to help you organize your ideas.

1. Look at the topics and add your own idea. Then choose one of the topics to write about.

How to make a good first impression on:	
a classmate	a college roommate
a teacher	a friend's parents
a new neighbor	your idea:

2. Think about your topic and write it here. Brainstorm some things you should do or should not do to make a good first impression. Make a list of dos and don'ts in the T-chart below.

My topic: _____

Dos	Don'ts

B. PLAN Follow these steps to plan your paragraph.

1. Look at the Dos and Don'ts you wrote in Activity A on page 25. Circle three ideas you want to use in your paragraph. These are your subtopics.

2. Brainstorm specific examples and reasons for your paragraph. Use ideas from Reading 1, Reading 2, and the unit video to help support your subtopics.

iQ RESOURCES Go online to download and complete the outline for your "how to" paragraph. *Resources > Writing Tools > Unit 1 > Outline*

C. WRITE Use your planning notes to write your paragraph.

1. Write your "how to" paragraph on making a good first impression. Be sure to include a topic sentence, supporting sentences, and a concluding sentence.

2. Look at the Self-Assessment checklist below to guide your writing.

iQ PRACTICE Go online to the Writing Tutor to write your assignment. *Practice > Unit 1 > Activity 14*

REVISE AND EDIT

iQ RESOURCES Go online to download the peer review worksheet. *Resources > Writing tools > Unit 1 > Peer Review Worksheet*

A. PEER REVIEW Read your partner's paragraph. Then use the peer review worksheet. Discuss the review with your partner.

B. REWRITE Based on your partner's review, revise and rewrite your paragraph.

C. EDIT Complete the Self-Assessment checklist as you prepare to write the final draft of your paragraph. Be prepared to hand in your work or discuss it in class.

SELF-ASSESSMENT	Yes	No
Does the paragraph have a strong topic sentence and concluding sentence?	☐	☐
Are there three subtopics with specific details?	☐	☐
Does the paragraph include conditionals? Are they used correctly?	☐	☐
Are all words used in their correct form?	☐	☐
Does the paragraph include vocabulary from the unit?	☐	☐
Did you check the paragraph for punctuation, spelling, and grammar?	☐	☐

D. REFLECT Discuss these questions with a partner or group.

1. What is something new you learned in this unit?

2. Look back at the Unit Question—How do you make a good first impression? Is your answer different now than when you started the unit? If yes, how is it different? Why?

iQ PRACTICE Go to the online discussion board to discuss the questions. *Practice > Unit 1 > Activity 15*

TRACK YOUR SUCCESS

iQ PRACTICE Go online to check the words and phrases you have learned in this unit. *Practice > Unit 1 > Activity 16*

Check (✓) the skills you learned. If you need more work on a skill, refer to the page(s) in parentheses.

CRITICAL THINKING ☐ I can identify a causal chain (p. 9)

READING ☐ I can identify main ideas and supporting details. (p. 10)

VOCABULARY ☐ I can use the dictionary to identify word forms. (p. 17)

WRITING ☐ I can organize and develop a paragraph. (pp. 19 and 21)

GRAMMAR ☐ I can use real conditionals. (p. 23)

OBJECTIVE ▶ ☐ I can gather information and ideas to write a paragraph on how to make a good first impression.

2

Nutritional Science

CRITICAL THINKING	making Inferences
READING	previewing a text
VOCABULARY	using context to understand words
WRITING	using descriptive adjectives
GRAMMAR	use and placement of adjectives

What makes food attractive?

A. Discuss these questions with your classmates.

1. What kinds of food do you eat every day?

2. What kinds of food do you eat on special occasions?

3. Look at the photo. Do you think how food looks—
   its presentation—affects how it tastes? Explain.

B. Listen to *The Q Classroom* online. Then answer these questions.

1. Yuna says that homemade food tastes the best. Why does homemade
   food taste better than prepared food?

2. Felix believes foods with too much sugar and fat cause
   weight problems. In contrast, what kinds of food do you
   think help people lose weight?

iQ PRACTICE Go to the online discussion board to discuss the
Unit Question with your classmates. *Practice > Unit 2 > Activity 1*

**UNIT
OBJECTIVE**

Read the articles and gather information and ideas to write a descriptive paragraph
about your favorite dish.

READING 1

Knowing Your Tastes

You are going to read an article from a food magazine about why people like and dislike certain foods. Use the article to gather information and ideas for your Unit Assignment.

PREVIEW THE READING

A. PREVIEW Read the title and headings. Then look at the pictures. The author has two main reasons for writing the article. Check (✓) the two reasons.

☐ to describe different kinds of foods

☐ to compare different kinds of tasters

☐ to argue why people should eat well

☐ to give advice about people's food choices

☐ to explain the causes of overeating

B. QUICK WRITE What is an important food or dish in your culture? Write for 5–10 minutes in response. Be sure to use this section for your Unit Assignment.

C. VOCABULARY Check (✓) the words you know. Then work with a partner to locate each word in the reading. Use clues to help define the words you don't know. Check your definitions in the dictionary.

at risk *(prep. phr.)*	**identify** *(v.)* 🔑 OPAL	**sensitive** *(adj.)* 🔑 OPAL
balanced *(adj.)* 🔑 OPAL	**likely** *(adj.)* 🔑 OPAL	**system** *(n.)* 🔑 OPAL
be made up of *(v. phr.)*	**recognize** *(v.)* 🔑 OPAL	**typically** *(adv.)* 🔑 OPAL

🔑 Oxford 3000™ words   **OPAL** Oxford Phrasal Academic Lexicon

iQ PRACTICE Go online to listen and practice your pronunciation.
Practice > Unit 2 > Activity 2

WORK WITH THE READING

 A. INVESTIGATE Read the article and gather information about what makes food taste good.

KNOWING YOUR TASTES

Food Likes and Dislikes

1   Why do some people love spicy food and others hate it? Why do many people dislike broccoli? Why do some people want sweets all the time? Human taste is not as simple as liking or disliking something. The kind of tongue you have can affect your food choices—and your health.

How the Tongue Works

2   The human tongue **is made up of** a group of muscles and taste buds that work together to **recognize** taste. The average adult tongue has 10,000 taste buds, which are tiny bumps located on the tongue. Tiny hairs on the end of the taste buds tell us whether food is sweet, sour, bitter, or salty. The taste buds send messages to the brain as chemicals from the food enter the nose. Together, the taste buds and nose tell the brain exactly what the tongue is tasting. This complex **system** helps humans survive by recognizing which foods are safe and which might be dangerous.

Nontasters, Medium Tasters, Supertasters

3   Although all humans have taste buds, we do not all have the same number of them. *Medium tasters* **typically** have 10,000 taste buds. These "average tasters" make up about 50 percent of the world population. *Nontasters*, 25 percent of the population, have half the number of taste buds as medium tasters. The remaining 25 percent are *supertasters*. Supertasters have four to six times as many taste buds as nontasters and twice as many as medium tasters (see Figure 1). Research shows that supertasters are more **likely** to be women and from Asia, Africa, and South America.

Different Worlds for Different Tasters

4   Supertasters live in a very colorful world of tastes, nontasters live in a gray world, and medium tasters are somewhere between the two. Supertasters think that a lot of foods are too strong. In addition to having more taste buds, supertasters are born with a gene[1] that makes them **sensitive** to bitter foods. Consequently, they dislike broccoli, cauliflower, grapefruit, and even coffee. With more taste buds, they can more easily feel fatty foods in their mouths. As a result, they stay away from high-fat food items like French fries and sweets. They are also very sensitive to pain on the tongue, so they avoid spicy food. Nontasters, on the other hand, experience fewer tastes in general, so they can enjoy hot foods like chili and pepper with much less pain.

[1] **gene:** a part of a cell in a living thing that decides its characteristics

...rs, Nontasters, and Diet

...ans avoid foods that taste bad and eat
...ve them pleasure. Since supertasters avoid
...ts and vegetables, their diets are sometimes not
...ced, which could put them more **at risk** for certain
...ypes of cancers. However, they also dislike fatty and
sweet foods, so they tend to be thinner and at lower risk
for heart disease and diabetes[2]. In contrast, nontasters
like foods high in fat because their tongues do not react
negatively to them. All people should pay attention to
what they eat, but nontasters and supertasters must
be more aware of the foods they are consuming or
avoiding and find other ways to make up the difference.

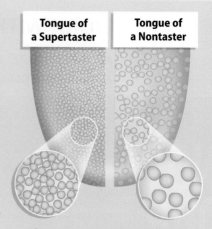

Tongue of a Supertaster	Tongue of a Nontaster

Figure 1 Supertasters have many more taste buds than nontasters.

What Kind of Taster Are You?

6   If you can **identify** which kind of taster you are, you will be able to make more educated
choices about your diet. This simple test can show whether you are a nontaster, medium
taster, or supertaster. Put a small amount of blue food coloring on your tongue. Take a piece
of notebook paper (the kind with three holes punched out), and put one of the holes over
your tongue. Your taste buds will look like little pink bumps on your blue tongue. Count how
many bumps you see in the hole. If there are 5 bumps or fewer, you are a nontaster. If there
are 30 or more, you are a supertaster. If there are between 5 and 30, you're a medium taster.

[2] **diabetes:** a serious disease in which a person's body cannot control the level of sugar in the body

**VOCABULARY
SKILL REVIEW**
In Unit 1, you learned
how to identify word
forms with a dictionary.
Look at all the words in
the sentences. Which
words are adjectives?
Which words are nouns
used like adjectives?

B. VOCABULARY Complete each sentence with the vocabulary from
Reading 1. You may need to change the form of some of the words.

8 at risk *(prep. phr.)*	6 identify *(v.)*	9 sensitive *(adj.)*
7 balanced *(adj.)*	4 likely *(adj.)*	3 system *(n.)*
be made up of *(v. phr.)* 2	recognize *(v.)* 1	typically *(adv.)* 5

1. I did not _____ the taste of the cake at first. It took me a minute
to realize that it tasted like blackberries.

2. Water _____ hydrogen and oxygen.

3. The human digestive _____ includes the mouth and stomach.
It helps to change the food we eat into energy.

4. People who don't eat well are more _____ to get sick than
people with healthy diets.

5. People who eat healthy foods and exercise _____ have fewer
health problems than people who don't.

6. The police used a photograph to _____ the man who stole Anita's wallet.

7. Most health experts agree that a(n) _____ diet should include different types of foods, such as meat, fruits, vegetables, bread, and cheese.

8. People who don't eat well are _____ of getting sick.

9. Abdullah's teeth are very _____ to cold, so he usually drinks water at room temperature.

iQ PRACTICE Go online for more practice with the vocabulary.
Practice > Unit 2 > Activity 3

C. IDENTIFY Circle the answer to each question.

1. What is the main idea of the article?

   a. As a rule, humans eat foods that taste good and avoid foods that taste bad.

   b. The kind of taster you are can affect your food choices and health.

   c. Supertasters live in a colorful world of taste, but nontasters live in a gray world.

   d. Supertasters have about 20,000 taste buds, double the amount that medium tasters have.

2. Which statement is true about taste buds?

   a. They send messages to the tongue.

   b. The average person has 5,000 taste buds.

   c. They are large bumps on the tongue.

   d. They tell the brain how food tastes.

3. Which statement is true about the number of taste buds a person has?

   a. How many taste buds you have has no effect on taste.

   b. The number of taste buds you have can cause you to like or dislike certain foods.

   c. The more taste buds you have, the more you enjoy spicy foods.

   d. People with a lot of taste buds never eat fruits or vegetables.

4. Which statement is true about the three different kinds of tasters?

   a. Finding out what kind of taster you are can help you make important decisions about your diet.

   b. Supertasters are more likely to be men from Asia, Africa, and South America.

   c. You need a complex test to show you what kind of taster you are.

   d. Unlike nontasters and supertasters, medium tasters do not have to care about the kinds of food they eat.

D. EXPLAIN Answer the questions. Write the paragraph number where the answer is found. Then discuss your answers with a partner.

1. What four tastes can taste buds identify? Paragraph: 2

_____

2. How many taste buds do nontasters have? Paragraph: ____

_____

3. Who is more likely to be a supertaster, a woman from Italy or a woman from Korea? Paragraph: ____

_____

4. What types of foods do supertasters avoid? Paragraph: ____

_____

5. Why should supertasters and nontasters pay close attention to the foods they eat? Paragraph: ____

_____

_____

_____

E. IDENTIFY Read these sentences from Reading 1. Then answer the questions. Find the sentences in the reading to help you.

1. (Paragraph 3) Although all humans have taste buds, we do not all have the same number of **them**.

   Who or what does *them* refer to?

   a. humans   b. taste buds   c. nontasters

2. (Paragraph 4) Consequently, **they** dislike broccoli, cauliflower, grapefruit, and even coffee.

   Who or what does *they* refer to?

   a. foods   b. medium tasters   c. supertasters

3. (Paragraph 4) **They** are also very sensitive to pain on the tongue, so **they** avoid spicy food.

   Who or what does *they* refer to?

   a. spicy food   b. supertasters   c. medium tasters

4. (Paragraph 5) However, **they** also dislike fatty and sweet foods, so **they** tend to be thinner and at lower risk for heart disease and diabetes.

Who or what does *they* refer to?

a. nontasters   b. medium tasters   c. supertasters

5. (Paragraph 5) In contrast, nontasters like foods high in fat because their tongues do not react negatively to **them**.

Who or what does *them* refer to?

a. high-fat foods   b. nontasters   c. taste buds

CRITICAL THINKING STRATEGY

Making inferences

When you **make inferences**, you are using your knowledge to think beyond the ideas that the author states in the text. Inferring means analyzing the information that is provided in a text to find out other information that was not given to you. In other words, you are looking for ideas that are suggested by the author, but not directly stated.

iQ PRACTICE   Go online to watch the Critical Thinking Video and check your comprehension. *Practice ⟩ Unit 2 ⟩ Activity 4*

F. INTERPRET Answer the questions. Then compare your answers with a partner.

1. Medium tasters have about 10,000 taste buds. How many taste buds do supertasters have?

_____

2. Can people decide to be a supertaster? Why or why not?

_____

3. Supertasters do not enjoy bitter foods or foods high in fat. They also dislike sweet foods. What kinds of foods do you think supertasters like to eat?

_____

4. Nontasters like spicy foods and high-fat foods. What kinds of health risks do you think nontasters have because of their diet?

_____

WRITE WHAT YOU THINK

A. DISCUSS Discuss the questions in a group.

1. Do you think you are a nontaster, medium taster, or supertaster? Why?

2. What foods do you really like or dislike? Choose one food and describe what you like or dislike about it.

3. In addition to the type of tasters they are, what are other possible reasons why people like certain foods and don't like others?

WRITING TIP
Remember to use your topic sentence to state your main idea.

B. COMPOSE Choose one of the questions from Activity A and write a paragraph in response. Look back at your Quick Write on page 30 as you think about what you learned.

READING SKILL Previewing a text

Previewing means looking through a text quickly to find the topic and main ideas before you read the whole text. Previewing gives you a general understanding of the reading first, which will help you when you read the whole text from beginning to end. When you preview, the goal is to predict what the text is going to talk about.

Previewing usually includes these steps:

- reading the title and headings
- looking at the photographs and pictures
- reading the first and last paragraphs

After you preview a text, you should be able to answer these questions:

- What is the topic of the reading?
- What ideas are discussed in the reading?

A. IDENTIFY Look at Reading 2. Follow these steps as you preview the text.

Step 1: Read the title and headings.

1. What is the title of the reading? _____

2. There are three headings. What are they?

   The Rise of the Food Pic; _____

   _____

Step 2: Look at the photographs. What are they of?

_____

Step 3: Read the first and last paragraphs. Read them quickly. Underline the topic sentence of each paragraph.

B. RECOGNIZE What is the topic of the reading?

_____

C. RESTATE What ideas are discussed in the reading?

_____

_____

iQ PRACTICE Go online for more practice previewing a text.
Practice > Unit 2 > Activity 5

iQ PRACTICE Go online for additional reading and comprehension.
Practice > Unit 2 > Activity 6

READING 2

Eating with Our Eyes

OBJECTIVE ▶

You are going to read a magazine article about food photography. Use the article to gather information and ideas for your Unit Assignment.

PREVIEW THE READING

A. PREVIEW What do you already know about this topic? Share your ideas with a partner.

ACADEMIC LANGUAGE
The corpus shows that phrases like _in terms of_, _in relation to_, and **with regard to** are often used in academic writing to specify a topic.

⌐ **OPAL**
Oxford Phrasal Academic Lexicon

B. QUICK WRITE Do you post pictures of food you eat on social media? Why or why not? Write for 5–10 minutes in response. Be sure to use this section for your Unit Assignment.

C. VOCABULARY Check (✓) the words you know. Use a dictionary to define any new or unknown words. Then discuss how the words will relate to the unit with a partner.

arrange _(v.)_ 🔑	in terms of _(prep. phr.)_ OPAL
artistic _(adj.)_ 🔑	method _(n.)_ 🔑 OPAL
be willing to _(v. phr.)_	occasion _(n.)_ 🔑
identical _(adj.)_ OPAL	principle _(n.)_ 🔑 OPAL
influence _(v.)_ 🔑 OPAL	status symbol _(n.)_

🔑 Oxford 3000™ words   **OPAL** Oxford Phrasal Academic Lexicon

iQ PRACTICE Go online to listen and practice your pronunciation.
Practice > Unit 2 > Activity 7

A. **INVESTIGATE** Read the article and gather information about what makes food attractive.

EATING WITH OUR EYES

Food that is neatly organized appears tastier.

THE RISE OF THE FOOD PIC

1   If you have ever shared a picture of a beautiful plate of food online, you're not alone. On Instagram alone, over 75 million pictures of people's favorite dishes are viewable online, and that number grows exponentially[1] every day. And this happens even though nobody else but you gets to actually taste the food!

2   Since the introduction of social media, posting pictures of the food we consume has become a normal pastime[2]. Sometimes it's a dish from a special **occasion**, like a birthday or holiday. Other times it's an amazing bowl of soup you tried at a new restaurant. And lots of times it's nothing special at all—in fact, there are more posts of pizza on Instagram than any other food! Over 17 million pictures of #pizza, in fact!

3   So, why exactly are people so addicted to posting food photos? One reason is because it says something about who we are. Posting a picture of broccoli and rice tells your friends and the world that you lead a healthy lifestyle. The food we eat can also be **a status symbol**. Showing everyone that you enjoyed lobster at a fancy restaurant suggests you have money, for example. **In terms of** food, a picture is more than just a picture. In fact, studies have shown that the better the picture, the tastier the food is!

[1]**exponentially:** used to say that a rate of increase is getting faster and faster
[2]**pastime:** something that you enjoy doing when you are not working

THE TASTIEST FOOD PHOTOS

4   Since the rise of the food pic, researchers have been studying exactly why one plate of food looks more delicious than another. And they have confirmed what many chefs and restaurants already knew. Plating food in an orderly or **artistic** way makes it appear more delicious.

5   In a study at Montclair State University in New Jersey, people were asked how they felt about food that was **arranged** neatly compared to food that looked messy. The people believed that food that was plated nicely tasted better even though it used the same ingredients. They also expected to like the neatly plated food better, and they **were willing to** pay more for it (Zellner et al. 2011).

6   Another study from the University of Oxford produced similar results. People were asked to compare two different salads. The salads tasted exactly the same. They had the same ingredients—mushrooms, broccoli, peppers, and sauces—but they looked very different. One was designed to look like a famous painting; the other looked like a traditional salad. The result? People were more willing to pay more for the fancier salad. Eighteen percent said it was tastier even though the ingredients were **identical** (Michel et al. 2014).

GETTING THAT PERFECT PIC

7   So, the next time you post a picture of your favorite dish, remember that it's all about the presentation. And food experts have some specific advice about how to make it look more delicious.

8   For one, proper lighting is key. If you are using the camera on your phone, it's best not to use the flash because it can cause shadows. Experts say natural lighting makes food look better. If necessary, move the plate to a different place to get more natural light. It's also good for the light to come from the side, especially when the dish has several textures, such as a sandwich.

Dark foods look better on white plates.

9   Food photographers also believe in another **principle**. To them, there is beauty in contrasts. Therefore, food that is round, like an egg or an orange, will look better on a square plate. Conversely, square food will look tastier on a round plate because it will be more enhanced. You also need to think about the color of the plate. If your food is brightly colored, use a dark plate so that it stands out more. If it is darker food, like grilled meat, use a white plate (Spense 2014).

10   In all, the **method** you use to photograph your food will **influence** the way others feel about it. And if you're lucky, you'll make them want to taste your food even more!

References:

Michel, Charles, Carlos Velasco, Elia Gatti, and Charles Spence. 2014. "A taste of Kandinsky: assessing the influence of the artistic visual presentation of food on the dining experience." *Flavour Journal* 3(7): 1–10.

Spense, Charles, Betina Piqueras-FiszMan, Charles Michel, and Ophelia Deroy. 2014. "Plating manifesto (II): the art and science of plating." *Flavour Journal* 3(4): 1–12.

Zellner, Debra, Evan Siemers, Vincenzo Teran, Rebecca Conroy, Mia Lankford, Alexis Agrafiotis, Lisa Ambrose, and Paul Locher. 2011. "Neatness counts: How plating affects liking for the taste of food." *Appetite* 57(3): 642–648.

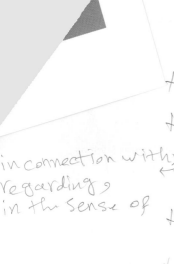

B. VOCABULARY Here are some words from Reading 2. Read the sentences. Then write each bold word next to the correct definition. You may need to change the form of some of the words.

1. I only eat meat on certain **occasions**, such as when I am invited to a friend's house for dinner. Otherwise, I prefer fruits and vegetables.

2. An expensive car like a Ferrari is a **status symbol** because it shows others how much money someone has.

in connection with,
regarding,
in the sense of

3. **In terms of** food preferences, supertasters are more likely to prefer foods that are not spicy. هنزبزاره

4. The film had a very interesting **artistic** quality. It used very low light, and the colors were all dark.

5. The chef **arranged** the vegetables on the plate to make them look like a beautiful butterfly.

6. Some people always order the same thing at their favorite restaurant. In contrast, more adventurous eaters **are willing to** try a new dish each time.

7. All the houses look **identical**, so it is difficult to tell them apart.

8. One **principle** of Chinese cooking is that food should be balanced. For example, a warm dish like fried rice might be eaten with a cool fruit like watermelon.

9. At many restaurants, grilling is a common **method** for cooking both vegetables and meats.

10. The kinds of food we eat as children can **influence** the foods we prefer as adults.

a. _____7_____ (adj.) similar in every detail

b. _____1_____ (n.) a particular time when something happens

c. _____8_____ (n.) a belief that is accepted as a reason for acting or thinking in a particular way

d. _____5_____ (v.) to put something in a particular order; to make something neat or attractive

e. _____9_____ (n.) a particular way of doing something

f. _____10_____ (v.) to affect the way someone thinks or behaves

g. _____3_____ (prep. phr.) relating to a specific topic or event

h. _____4_____ (adj.) connected with art or artists

i. _____6_____ (v. phr.) to be happy or ready to do something, without needing to be persuaded سنگاکردن

j. _____2_____ (n.) a possession that is a sign of someone's high status or wealth

iQ PRACTICE   Go online for more practice with the vocabulary.
Practice > Unit 2 > Activity 8

C. RESTATE Circle the main idea of the article.

a. The food photos people post online can suggest a lot about their status in society.

b. Millions of food photographs have been shared on social media sites such as Instagram.

c. Food photographers believe that dark foods look better when placed on white plates.

d. Food photos can influence people's opinions about food, taste, and social status.

D. IDENTIFY Read the main ideas. Write the paragraph number where they are found.

_____ 1. A study showed that people thought food was tastier when it looked like art.

_____ 2. It's common for people to post pictures of their food on social media.

_____ 3. A study showed that people thought food was tastier when it was arranged neatly.

_____ 4. Experts say that good lighting can make food look more delicious.

_____ 5. People post food photos to tell other people about their likes and lifestyle.

_____ 6. Food photographers believe that contrasting colors and shapes make food look tastier.

E. CATEGORIZE Write *T* (true) or *F* (false). Then correct each false statement to make it true according to the article.

_____ 1. There are over 75 million pictures of pizza on Instagram.

_____ 2. Posting a picture of broccoli and rice shows others you have money.

_____ 3. People are willing to pay more for food that looks tastier.

_____ 4. The study at Montclair State University asked people to compare salads.

_____ 5. Using the flash on your phone can make food look better.

_____ 6. When you take a picture of food, it's better for the light to come from the front.

_____ 7. An egg will look more attractive on a square plate.

_____ 8. Foods that are bright look better on a dark plate.

F. IDENTIFY Read these sentences from Reading 2. Then answer the questions. Find the sentences in the reading to help you.

1. (Paragraph 2) Other times **it's** an amazing bowl of soup you tried at a new restaurant.

   What does *it* refer to? _____

2. (Paragraph 4) And **they** have confirmed what many chefs and restaurants already knew.

   Who does *they* refer to? _____

3. (Paragraph 5) They also expected to like the neatly plated food better, and **they** were willing to pay more for it.

   Who does *they* refer to? _____

4. (Paragraph 6) Eighteen percent said **it** was tastier even though the ingredients were identical.

   What does *it* refer to? _____

5. (Paragraph 8) If you are using the camera on your phone, it's best not to use the flash because **it** can cause shadows.

   What does *it* refer to? _____

6. (Paragraph 9) To **them**, there is beauty in contrasts.

   Who does *them* refer to? _____

G. INTERPRET Check (✓) the statements you can infer from the reading.

☐ 1. Food photography would be less popular without social media.

☐ 2. People are more likely to post photos of food from a birthday than a holiday.

☐ 3. People post pictures of food from fancy restaurants to impress others.

☐ 4. It's unusual for people to like things that are more beautiful.

☐ 5. Many people do not know the right way to photograph food.

☐ 6. A piece of square bread would look better to people on a round plate.

H. COMPOSE Is it important to you for food to be presented in a neat or artistic way? Write a paragraph of 5–8 sentences in response.

WORK WITH THE VIDEO

A. PREVIEW Do you enjoy trying foods from other countries? Share your opinion with a partner.

VIDEO VOCABULARY

takeaway (adj.) food that you buy already cooked from a restaurant to eat somewhere else

profit (n.) the money that you make in a business or by selling things, after paying the costs involved

dish (n.) food prepared in a particular way as part of a meal

mix (n.) a combination of different people or things

iQ RESOURCES Go online to watch the video about local restaurants in London. *Resources > Video > Unit 2 > Unit Video*

B. IDENTIFY Watch the video two or three times. Then answer the questions.

1. Where is Peckham located?

_____

2. What kind of food does Jennifer's shop serve?

_____

3. When does Jennifer start cooking?

_____

4. What kinds of foods does Sally sell in her shop?

_____

5. What three "ingredients" make a great meal for people from Peckham?

_____

C. EXTEND Do you believe it is important for families to share at least one meal per day? Discuss your answer with a partner.

WRITE WHAT YOU THINK

SYNTHESIZE Think about Reading 1, Reading 2, and the unit video as you discuss these questions. Then choose one question and write a paragraph in response.

1. What makes food more attractive to you?

2. Which foods did you dislike as a child? Which foods do you dislike as an adult? Why do you think food preferences change as you get older?

3. Why does food make people feel good?

VOCABULARY SKILL Using context to understand words

Learning to read without stopping to look up new words can help you read faster and understand more. When reading, try to guess the meaning of a new word from **context**. Context refers to the other words and ideas in the sentence that are around the new word:

> A balanced diet usually means eating more fruits, vegetables, and grains and **consuming** fewer foods high in fat, sugar, and cholesterol.

The context around the word *consuming* suggests that the sentence is about what kinds of food to eat and not eat in order to have a balanced diet. Therefore, you can guess that *consuming* has a similar meaning to *eating*.

If you need to know what a word means, start by guessing from the context. If a sentence does not give enough context, then look the word up in the dictionary.

A. INTERPRET Read each sentence and try to answer the question that follows. (The bold words are for Activity B.)

1. People in every culture have their own ideas of what **constitutes** a balanced meal, whether it is tastes, menus, ingredients, eating habits, or nutritional benefits.

   What things can make a balanced meal?

   tastes, menus, ingredients, eating habits, and nutritional benefits

2. Pizza and lasagna are two famous **dishes** that can be found in most Italian restaurants.

   What foods are common in Italian restaurants?

   _____

3. Cultures might **view** balance differently—for example, according to the way a dish tastes or how a meal is prepared and served.

   In what ways might a culture look for balance in food?

   _____

4. Nontasters have a **taste** for sugary foods, which means they eat sweets more often than other people.

Why do nontasters eat sweets?

_____

5. French cheeses can have different **textures**, from soft cheeses like Brie to hard cheeses like cantal.

In what way can French cheeses differ?

_____

6. In traditional Chinese cooking, foods are in **harmony** when there is an equal amount of cool and warm foods together.

What foods work together in Chinese cooking?

_____

B. EXTEND Check (✓) the word or phrase that is closest in meaning to the bold word. Look at the word in context in Activity A.

1. **constitutes**
   - ☐ eats
   - ☑ makes

2. **dishes**
   - ☑ meals
   - ☐ tastes

3. **view**
   - ☑ think about
   - ☐ eliminate

4. **taste**
   - ☐ an idea
   - ☐ a liking

5. **textures**
   - ☑ ways that things feel
   - ☐ ways that things smell

6. **harmony**
   - ☐ a good recipe
   - ☑ a good combination

C. COMPOSE Choose four words from Activities A and B. Write a sentence using each word.

1. _____

2. _____

3. _____

4. _____

iQ PRACTICE Go online for more practice using context to understand words. *Practice ⟩ Unit 2 ⟩ Activity 9*

WRITING

OBJECTIVE ▶ At the end of this unit, you will write a paragraph about your favorite dish using descriptive adjectives. This paragraph will include specific information from the readings, the unit video, and your own ideas.

WRITING SKILL Using descriptive adjectives

Adjectives are words that describe nouns (*people, places, things,* and *ideas*). Writers use a lot of adjectives in order to make their descriptions both interesting and clear. They describe what they *see, hear, smell, taste, touch,* and *feel*. They create a picture with words so that readers can easily imagine or "see" what they are describing. Using **descriptive adjectives** in your writing will make it more interesting for the reader.

Non-descriptive: I ate a meal at a restaurant downtown.

Descriptive: I ate a **delicious**, **savory** meal at a **cozy French** restaurant downtown.

A. WRITING MODEL Read the model paragraph. Then answer the questions on page 47.

My Mother's Yorkshire Puddings

Whenever I think of my mother's cooking, I always remember her delicious Yorkshire puddings. Although I grew up in the United States, my mother often cooked dishes from her home country of England. She has always been an excellent cook, and one of her best recipes is called *Yorkshire pudding*, which is a traditional English pastry. It is a simple dish made with eggs, flour, and milk. My mother's Yorkshire puddings taste so good because they are light, crisp, and slightly sweet. She serves them with delicious warm gravy, but I prefer them sweet with strawberry jam.

They are very special because she only serves them on holidays. My sister and I always fight for the last one because they are so delicious. I have had many other people's Yorkshire puddings, but my mother's have always tasted better. Not only are hers homemade, but they also have a special taste that always makes me think of her. In addition, they make me remember my British ancestry and my mother's history. They help me connect to my past and to my family. Yorkshire pudding is such a simple and common English food, but it will always be special to me because of my mother.

1. What is the topic sentence? Underline it.

2. What is the concluding sentence? Underline it.

3. How does Yorkshire pudding taste? Write a sentence that describes the taste.

_____

4. What do Yorkshire puddings remind the author of?

_____

5. Circle the adjectives the writer uses to describe Yorkshire pudding.

B. CATEGORIZE Look at the author's brainstorming notes. Circle the ideas the author used. Cross out the ideas the author did not use.

eggs, flour, & milk   homemade

~~bake in the oven~~   British ancestry

crisp and sweet   my grandmother

golden brown   family

holidays   smell buttery

sweet with strawberry jam   New Year's Day

fight with sister

C. EXPLAIN Look again at the author's notes in Activity B. Why do you think the author used some of the ideas but not others?

D. WRITING MODEL Read the model paragraph. Check (✓) the best topic sentence on page 48. Then write it on the lines in the paragraph.

The Best Ceviche

_____

_____

Restaurants all over Lima serve this traditional South American seafood dish. Ceviche is a simple recipe made from fresh raw fish, shrimp, and other seafood. The seafood sits in fresh lemon or lime juice, which makes a broth and "cooks" the meat naturally. Hot chili peppers, raw onions, and a little salt are added to the sour juice to give ceviche its special flavor. The fish is cold and citrusy. Sliced limes and fresh cilantro often garnish the top, which makes the dish very colorful and appetizing. Sometimes people just have the broth as an appetizer because it is so delicious. Since Lima is located on the coast of the South Pacific Ocean, restaurants there have access to fresh seafood every morning, so the ceviche is always exceptional. I enjoy ceviche from Lima's famous restaurants, but it is also a common street food. People make their own ceviche and sell it on the streets of Lima. When I see fellow Peruvians enjoying their street ceviche while walking along city sidewalks, I feel very proud of my country and its food.

☐ Ceviche tastes best in the summer because it is cold and refreshing.

☐ Nothing tastes better than the ceviche in Lima, Peru.

☐ People in Lima, Peru, enjoy ceviche in restaurants and on the street.

☐ Lima, the capital of Peru, has many good seafood dishes.

E. IDENTIFY Fill in the adjectives the author uses in Activity D to describe the nouns.

1. _simple_ recipe   5. _____ limes

2. _____ chili peppers   6. _____ cilantro

3. _____ onions   7. _____ restaurants

4. _____ flavor

F. CREATE Write two of your own adjectives to describe each of these nouns from Activity D. Then compare your answers with a partner.

1. _traditional_ recipe   4. _____ limes

   _____   _____

2. _____ onions   5. _____ restaurants

   _____   _____

3. _____ flavor

   _____

iQ PRACTICE Go online for more practice with using descriptive adjectives.
Practice > Unit 2 > Activity 10

GRAMMAR Use and placement of adjectives

Adjectives are always singular. When two or more adjectives are used noun, they usually follow the order given in this chart.

Opinion/ Quality	Size	Age	Shape	Color	Origin	Material	Purpose
beautiful	big	old	round	yellow	Chinese	glass	serving
expensive	small	new	square	green	French	leather	running

Rosario lives in a **big old** house in the country.

We ate dinner at the **new French** restaurant in our neighborhood.

Ming gave Ella and Mike a **beautiful glass serving** dish as a gift.

Eduardo bought a pair of **expensive leather running** shoes.

We do not usually use more than three adjectives before a noun. We use two or three adjectives and then add additional descriptive phrases after the noun.

Leila wore a **beautiful green silk** skirt from India.

iQ RESOURCES Go online to watch the Grammar Skill Video.
Resources > Video > Unit 2 > Grammar Skill Video

A. COMPOSE Write a sentence about each topic with three adjectives from different categories. Use adjectives from the list on page 50 or your own ideas.

1. your favorite dessert _____

2. a member of your family _____

3. something you are wearing today _____

4. something you ate this week _____

5. a DVD or book you like _____

6. a restaurant you like _____

B. CATEGORIZE Work with a partner. Write each adjective in the correct column of the chart below.

American	friendly	metal	tasty
ancient	funny	modern	teenage
antique	glass	nice	traditional
Brazilian	~~hiking~~	Omani	triangular
ceramic	huge	orange	ugly
~~cheap~~	interesting	oval	uncomfortable
common	jogging	plastic	unusual
cotton	Korean	pretty	wedding
elderly	little	racing	wonderful
elegant	lovely	rectangular	wool
fashionable	medical	silk	writing

Opinion/Quality	*cheap,*
Size	
Age	
Shape	
Color	
Origin	
Material	
Kind/Purpose	*hiking,* what use for

iQ PRACTICE Go online for more practice with the use and placement of adjectives. *Practice ▸ Unit 2 ▸ Activities 11–12*

UNIT ASSIGNMENT **Write a descriptive paragraph**

OBJECTIVE ▶

In this assignment, you are going to write a descriptive paragraph about your favorite dish. As you prepare your paragraph, think about the Unit Question, "What makes food attractive?" Use information from Reading 1, Reading 2, the unit video, and your work in this unit to support your descriptive paragraph. Refer to the Self-Assessment checklist on page 52.

iQ PRACTICE Go online to the Writing Tutor to read a model descriptive paragraph. *Practice > Unit 2 > Activity 13*

PLAN AND WRITE

A. BRAINSTORM Follow these steps to help you organize your ideas.

1. Think about your favorite dish. Use these questions to help brainstorm ideas about your topic.

   a. What is the name of your dish? _____

   b. How would you describe your dish? What taste(s) and ingredients does it have? _____

   _____

   c. Does this dish have personal or cultural importance to you? Why?

   _____

   _____

   d. Who usually makes this dish for you? Is it easy or difficult to make? Why?

   _____

   _____

   e. How does the dish make you feel? _____

   _____

2. Write a topic sentence that names your dish and expresses your main idea.

   _____

   _____

   _____

3. List 8–10 adjectives that describe your dish. Think about how it looks and tastes.

   _____

   _____

B. PLAN Follow these steps to plan your paragraph.

1. Look at the ideas you wrote in Activity A on page 51. Circle your best ideas.

2. Look again at your ideas. Circle your best descriptive adjectives. Check the order. Look at the Grammar box chart on page 49 to help you.

iQ RESOURCES Go online to download and complete the outline for your descriptive paragraph. *Resources > Writing Tools > Unit 2 > Outline*

C. WRITE Use your planning notes to write your paragraph.

1. Write your paragraph describing your favorite dish. Be sure to use adjectives to make your description interesting, clear, and specific.

2. Look at the Self-Assessment checklist below to guide your writing.

iQ PRACTICE Go online to the Writing Tutor to write your assignment. *Practice > Unit 2 > Activity 14*

REVISE AND EDIT

iQ RESOURCES Go online to download the peer review worksheet. *Resources > Writing Tools > Unit 2 > Peer Review Worksheet*

A. PEER REVIEW Read your partner's paragraph. Then use the peer review worksheet. Discuss the review with your partner.

B. REWRITE Based on your partner's review, revise and rewrite your paragraph.

C. EDIT Complete the Self-Assessment checklist as you prepare to write the final draft of your paragraph. Be prepared to hand in your work or discuss it in class.

SELF-ASSESSMENT	Yes	No
Does the paragraph include descriptive adjectives?	☐	☐
Are the adjectives in the correct order?	☐	☐
Does the paragraph include vocabulary from the unit?	☐	☐

D. REFLECT Discuss these questions with a partner or group.

1. What is something new you learned in this unit?

2. Look back at the Unit Question—What makes food attractive? Is your answer different now than when you started the unit? If yes, how is it different? Why?

iQ PRACTICE Go to the online discussion board to discuss the questions. *Practice > Unit 2 > Activity 15*

TRACK YOUR SUCCESS

iQ PRACTICE Go online to check the words and phrases you have learned in this unit. *Practice > Unit 2 > Activity 16*

Check (✓) the skills you learned. If you need more work on a skill, refer to the page(s) in parentheses.

CRITICAL THINKING   ☐ I can make inferences. (p. 35)

READING   ☐ I can preview a text. (p. 36)

VOCABULARY   ☐ I can use context to understand words. (p. 44)

WRITING   ☐ I can use descriptive adjectives. (p. 46)

GRAMMAR   ☐ I can use adjectives in the correct order. (p. 49)

OBJECTIVE ▶   ☐ I can gather information and ideas to write a descriptive paragraph about my favorite dish.

3 Information Technology

CRITICAL THINKING	identifying advantages and disadvantages
READING	taking notes
VOCABULARY	synonyms
WRITING	writing a summary and a personal response
GRAMMAR	parallel structure

How has technology affected our lives?

A. Discuss these questions with your classmates.

1. How do you use technology in your daily life?

2. Look at the photo. What kind of technology is the child using? What is she doing?

B. Listen to *The Q Classroom* online. Then answer these questions.

1. Sophy says that technology has helped her keep in touch with her friends. What example does she give? Do you agree that technology helps you keep in touch? Why or why or not?

2. Sophy, Yuna, Felix, and Marcus find it hard to imagine life without technology. Do you feel the same way? Can you give an example?

iQ PRACTICE   Go to the online discussion board to discuss the Unit Question with your classmates. *Practice > Unit 3 > Activity 1*

UNIT OBJECTIVE

Read the articles and gather information and ideas to write a summary and a personal response paragraph about how technology has affected our lives.

READING

READING 1

OBJECTIVE ▶

Cars That Think

You are going to read an article from an automotive magazine about driverless cars. Use the article to gather information and ideas for your Unit Assignment.

PREVIEW THE READING

A. PREVIEW Read the title and the first sentence of each paragraph. What is the article's main purpose? Check (✓) your answer.

☐ to show why driverless cars will be too expensive to buy

☐ to suggest that people should buy driverless cars

☐ to discuss advantages and disadvantages of driverless cars

B. QUICK WRITE Would you feel comfortable in a driverless car? Why or why not? Write for 5–10 minutes in response. Be sure to use this section for your Unit Assignment.

C. VOCABULARY Check (✓) the words you know. Then work with a partner to locate each word in the reading. Use clues to help define the words you don't know. Check your definitions in the dictionary.

ACADEMIC LANGUAGE

The corpus shows that *benefits of* is often used in academic writing.
. . . the benefits of smartphones include . . .
. . . is one of the benefits of driverless cars . . .

_____ OPAL
Oxford Phrasal Academic Lexicon

data *(n.)* ⚷ OPAL	obey *(v.)* ⚷	respond *(v.)* ⚷ OPAL
limitation *(n.)* OPAL	obstacle *(n.)*	sense *(v.)* ⚷ OPAL
manufacturer *(n.)*	occur *(v.)* ⚷ OPAL	the benefits of *(n. phr.)* OPAL

⚷ Oxford 3000™ words   OPAL Oxford Phrasal Academic Lexicon

iQ PRACTICE Go online to listen and practice your pronunciation.
Practice › Unit 3 › Activity 2

A. INVESTIGATE Read the article and gather information about how technology has affected our lives.

CARS THAT THINK

1   Thanks to modern technology, humans have less to do. Machines make our coffee in the morning and clean our dishes. Robots do the vacuuming, mop the floors, and mow our yards hands-free. But what would it be like if machines drove our cars for us? What if cars could drive us to work while we read the newspaper or worked on the computer? This may sound like science fiction[1]. In fact, driverless cars are already on the roads and could soon end up at a dealer near you.

2   Cars today already think for us. GPS navigation systems can give people directions without looking at a map. Sensors[2] built into cars sound an alarm if drivers get too close to a person or another vehicle. Cameras can see for us at night and steer cars around **obstacles** to avoid accidents. By using GPS, sensors, and cameras together, cars can now park themselves and control drivers when they're about to make a dangerous turn. Now car companies are building driverless cars that will do all of this, and much more.

3   Driverless cars use a lot of the same technological features to make hands-free driving possible. A prototype[3] driverless car has sensors and cameras to give the car a 360-degree "eye" to **sense** its full environment. The sensors can "see" turns, red lights, stop signs, and other cars. Its computer uses GPS and other **data** to drive the car safely to its destination. All you need to do is tell it where to go and how you want to drive. Select "cautious," and it will **obey** the speed limit. Or choose "aggressive" and drive faster.

4   According to car **manufacturers, the benefits of** hands-free are significant. For one, driverless cars can improve safety. In the United States, over 90 percent of car accidents are the result of human error. Drivers can make bad judgments, get sleepy, and run red lights, but robots don't. In a hands-free car, people can **respond** to email without worrying

[1] **science fiction:** books, movies, etc., about events that take place in the future
[2] **sensor:** equipment that can detect certain sounds and movements
[3] **prototype:** a model or design of something from which other forms are developed
[4] **automated:** operated by machine, without needing people

Driverless cars may be too "polite" on the highway, where many people speed. A car that is following the speed limit could cause more accidents. In addition, if an accident does **occur**, who is to blame? Do you blame the driver? The car? The car manufacturer? Driving laws are written for human drivers, not robots. Therefore, countries will have to decide who is responsible and write new laws, which won't be easy.

about hitting another car. Also, driverless cars would use less fuel. They don't need to be as heavy because they are less likely to crash.

5   Although driverless cars sound perfect, there are **limitations**. For instance, automated[4] cars cannot anticipate the unexpected like humans can. They might not recognize when a police officer tells traffic to stop or pull off the road.

6   In the end, consumers will decide if driverless cars are to become the cars of the future. Some might not want to give up control of the wheel. Others may want driving to be as easy as making coffee. Car manufacturers already believe in the driverless car, and today even Uber is testing its own cars for its popular ridesharing program. Prototype driverless cars have already driven millions of miles accident-free, but only time will tell if consumers believe they should.

B. VOCABULARY Complete each sentence with the vocabulary from Reading 1.

data *(n.)*	obey *(v.)*	respond *(v.)*
limitation *(n.)*	obstacle *(n.)*	sense *(v.)*
manufacturer *(n.)*	occur *(v.)*	the benefits of *(n. phr.)*

VOCABULARY SKILL REVIEW

In Unit 1, you learned how to identify word forms with a dictionary. Circle the nouns and underline the verbs in Activity B.

1. Even though cars have headlights, accidents are more likely to _____occur_____ at night because drivers can't see as well.

2. The police expect drivers to _____obey_____ the speed limit on highways. If drivers go too fast, they may get a ticket.

3. In many buildings, the lights can _____sense_____ when people enter a room, and they turn on by themselves.

4. If my computer turns off by accident, I don't worry about losing my work because the _____data_____ is already saved.

manufacture
تصنيع

manufacture
تصنيع

5. The car _____ _manufacture_ _____ has decided to build a car that runs on
   gasoline and electricity because its customers want vehicles that use
   less fuel.

6. My boss expects me to ___ _respond_ ___ to his emails right away.
   If he doesn't hear from me, he gets upset.

7. Having flexibility and enjoying comfort are two of ~~the benefits of~~
   driving to work. But a disadvantage is getting stuck in traffic.

8. If you don't pay for a membership to the website, you can't read all the articles.
   There's a(n) ___ _limitation_ ___ on how much information you can access
   without paying.

9. Sand is a real ___ _obstacle_ ___ when driving in the desert. It makes it
   difficult to control the speed and direction of the car.

iQ PRACTICE Go online for more practice with the vocabulary.
Practice > Unit 3 > Activity 3

C. **IDENTIFY** Read the sentences. Then number them in the order that the
   ideas appear in the article.

_4_ 1. Driverless cars are not perfect machines.   _5 Paragraph_
_1_ 2. Today's cars can already do many tasks automatically. _2 Paragraph_
_3_ 3. Car manufacturers believe hands-free driving has advantages. _4_
_5_ 4. The future success of driverless cars will depend on consumers. _6_
_2_ 5. New cars and driverless cars use similar technology. _3_

D. **INTERPRET** Circle the main idea of the article.

a. Modern technology is making daily tasks easier for people to do.

b. Car manufacturers say that driverless cars will use less gasoline.

c. Driverless cars might cause more accidents on roads and highways.

(d.) In the near future, driverless cars may change the way people drive.

E. EXPLAIN Answer the questions. Write the paragraph number where the answer is found. Then discuss your answers with a partner.

1. How would driverless cars save fuel? Paragraph: _4_

   They can be lighter because they are less likely to crash.

2. How many miles have the prototype cars already driven accident-free?
   Paragraph: ____

   _____

3. What do modern cars use to park themselves? Paragraph: ____

   _____

4. What limitations do driverless cars have? Paragraph: ____

   _____

   _____

   _____

F. CATEGORIZE Read the statements. Write *F* (fact) or *O* (opinion).

____ 1. Using a driverless car has several important benefits.

____ 2. Driverless cars are safer than traditional cars.

____ 3. Hands-free driving requires modern technology.

____ 4. Over 90 percent of car accidents in the U.S. are due to human error.

____ 5. Driverless cars use sensors and GPS to navigate. F

____ 6. Hands-free driving sounds like science fiction.

____ 7. Driving laws are not written for robots. F

____ 8. It will be difficult for countries to write new laws for driverless cars.

CRITICAL THINKING STRATEGY

Identifying advantages and disadvantages

It is important to **identify** the **advantages** and **disadvantages** of a topic as you read. Using a chart can help you organize ideas into advantages and disadvantages. This will help you to compare and evaluate them better when writing and help you make a more informed opinion about the topic.

iQ PRACTICE Go online to watch the Critical Thinking Video and check your comprehension. *Practice > Unit 3 > Activity 4*

G. CATEGORIZE Complete the graphic organizer using your own words. Identify the advantages and disadvantages of driverless cars. Write the paragraph number where the answer is found.

Advantages of driverless cars	Disadvantages of driverless cars
• _They can help people stay safe._ _use less fuel_ Paragraph: _4_	• _They can't anticipate unexpected_ _things like people can._ Paragraph: _5_
• _human have less to do_ Paragraph: _1_	• _too polite – driving laws_ Paragraph: _5_
• _People drive without looking_ _a map — cameras see at night_ Paragraph: _2_	• _____ Paragraph: ____
• _____ Paragraph: _3_	• _____ Paragraph: ____

[handwritten margin notes:]
avoid accident
car themselves
control drivers

hand free driving
360-degree eye
obey speed limit
strike ?

H. DISCUSS Work with a partner. Discuss how the advantages and disadvantages of driverless cars would affect transportation in the future.

iQ PRACTICE Go online for additional reading and comprehension.
Practice > Unit 3 > Activity 5

WRITE WHAT YOU THINK

A. DISCUSS Discuss the questions in a group.

1. Why do you think car companies want to make driverless cars?

2. Compare and evaluate the advantages and disadvantages of driverless cars. Would you consider buying a driverless car? Why or why not?

B. COMPOSE Choose one of the questions from Activity A and write a paragraph in response. Look back at your Quick Write on page 56 as you think about what you learned.

READING SKILL Taking notes

Taking notes while you are reading will help you become a more active reader. To take notes, write on the text and next to the text. Your notes should help you identify important ideas. You should:

- underline or highlight topics and main ideas
- underline supporting details and the most important words and phrases
- focus on content words like nouns, verbs, and adjectives
- summarize the main idea of each paragraph in the margin—don't use complete sentences

Reviewing your notes can help you remember important concepts. Use your notes to prepare for a class or an exam.

A. ANALYZE Read the second paragraph of Reading 1 below. Look at the student's notes in blue. Then discuss the questions with a partner.

"Smart" cars think for us

Cars today already think for us. GPS navigation systems can give people directions without looking at a map. Sensors built into cars sound an alarm if drivers get too close to a person or another vehicle. Cameras can see for us at night and steer cars around obstacles to avoid accidents. By using GPS, sensors, and cameras together, cars can now park themselves and control drivers when they're about to make a dangerous turn. Now car companies are building driverless cars that will do all of this, and much more.

1. What types of words did the student underline?

_____

_____

2. Look at the words and ideas the student did not underline. Why are they less important?

_____

_____

3. Look at the note in the margin. What does the note summarize?

_____

_____

4. What is the main idea of the paragraph? How do you know?

_____

_____

_____

B. RESTATE Reread Reading 1. Take notes using ideas from the Reading Skill box and Activity A on pages 62–63. Then compare your notes with a partner.

iQ PRACTICE Go online for more practice with taking notes.
Practice > Unit 3 > Activity 6

READING 2

Classrooms without Walls

OBJECTIVE ▶

You are going to read an article from a newspaper about using tablet computers in schools. Use the article to gather information and ideas for your Unit Assignment.

PREVIEW THE READING

A. PREVIEW Read the title and look at the photographs. Then read the first sentence of each paragraph. What do you think the title means by "classroom without walls"?

B. QUICK WRITE Do you think computers help children learn better? Why or why not? Write for 5–10 minutes in response. Be sure to use this section for your Unit Assignment.

C. VOCABULARY Work with a partner to find the words in the reading. Circle clues in the text that help you understand the meaning of each word. Then use a dictionary to define any unknown words.

adapt *(v.)* 🔊 OPAL	global *(adj.)* 🔊 OPAL	monitor *(v.)* 🔊 OPAL
digital *(adj.)* 🔊 OPAL	in favor of *(prep. phr.)*	reliable *(adj.)* 🔊 OPAL
discover *(v.)* 🔊	interactive *(adj.)* OPAL	revolutionize *(v.)*
feedback *(n.)* 🔊		

🔊 Oxford 3000™ words   **OPAL** Oxford Phrasal Academic Lexicon

iQ PRACTICE Go online to listen and practice your pronunciation.
Practice > Unit 3 > Activity 7

WORK WITH THE READING

 A. INVESTIGATE Read the article and gather information about how technology has affected our lives.

Classrooms without Walls

1   Ali and his classmates sit next to each other in an eighth-grade science class in Saudi Arabia. They are not listening to their teacher or taking notes in their science journals. Ali is watching a video about cells on his iPad. Other students are using an app to design their own science experiment. When they need help, they type a quick message to their teacher, who **monitors** them from his computer.

2   In the U.S., young students are learning about world geography not through maps but through real people online. Using the Global Book Series app, schoolchildren from other countries create and upload presentations about their countries with photos and videos. American students then access this **digital** library on their tablets and go on tours of cities in Russia, Belgium, and New Zealand from people who actually live there. They watch them, they hear them, and the places feel much more real than maps ever would. In return, American students then share their own tours of cities in the U.S. *Am students are using digital tech to learn about Geography by communicating with students around the world*

3   In today's world, tablet computers are **revolutionizing** education. More schools are using tablets instead of paper or books. Many governments predict the best jobs will require students to have strong computer skills. They want their students to be prepared for the future, where jobs in science and technology will dominate[1]. Countries around the world are investing millions in technology for education, and putting tablets in children's hands is one step toward their goal. *Countries Preparing students for future by investing in tablets for education*

4   Why are more and more educators **in favor of** tablet education? According to them, one of the biggest advantages is tablets allow students to be more creative. Experts agree that tablets should not just be for note-taking. Instead, they should be used to help students make their studies and their ideas come to life.

5   As an example, students in a history class in the United Arab Emirates (UAE) are using an app to **discover** and "rebuild" an ancient city. To start, they take a video tour of the ancient city of Petra. With tablet technology, they can "walk through" it as if they were really there. Next, they use an app to design their own city. Finally, with special software[2], they turn their designs into a presentation and share them instantly on their screens. The students use creativity to solve their own problems. Experts believe this motivates students to learn more.

Children using tablets in the classroom

[1] **dominate:** to control or have a lot of influence over something or somebody
[2] **software:** the programs used by a computer for doing particular jobs

6   Another advantage of tablet education is that learning is more **interactive**. Without tablets, students are limited to communicating with their teacher and the other students in their classroom. With tablets, they have access to a much larger, **global** community. In Canada, teacher Kristen Wideen works with another teacher in Singapore. Their students have used Twitter and Skype to share math problems and tweet about tadpoles[3]. The benefit is their students get a more global perspective than they would with just a book. They have a much bigger audience for their ideas.

7   Studies have shown that having tablets in the classroom can improve students' test scores. A study of 266 kindergarten students in the United States showed that students with tablets scored higher on every reading test, compared to students without them (Bebell et al. 2012). Another study in California reported that middle school students with iPads did 20 percent better on their math tests, compared to students who just used a textbook (Bonnington 2012). Part of this is because tablets allow teachers to help students instantly. When students' scores on an online test are low, teachers can direct them right away to a video or website for extra instruction. Students can also email or text their teachers for help and get instant **feedback**.

8   Still, no technology is perfect. Many students are often expected to complete tablet assignments at home. One problem is that not all families have Internet access. Other times, Internet connections are slow or stop working. This can put children at a disadvantage. For this reason, governments around the world are also investing millions in fast, **reliable** Internet for schools and cities, but this will take time.

9   For teachers, another disadvantage is that students can get easily distracted[4] on their tablets. After they complete their assignments, some students end up playing a game or texting a friend. They stop concentrating on the teacher and the classroom. This can be frustrating to teachers. It can make students miss important information. Too much distraction can also have a negative impact on students' grades.

10   How can these kinds of problems be solved? For one, teachers are going to need more training in using tablet instruction. Second, schools will have to make sure that children are accessing the right content at the right time. And parents must also learn to **adapt** to technology they never had in school. But, if students, parents, and teachers can work together, the "classroom without walls" could become the classroom of the future and prepare children even better for our connected, digital world.

References

Bebell, Damian, Sue Dorris, and Miko Muir. 2012. "Emerging results from the nation's first kindergarten implementation of iPads." Research Summary. Auburn: Auburn School Department.

Bonnington, Christina. January 20, 2012. "IPad a solid education tool, study reports." Retrieved from https://www.wired.com/2012/01/ipad-educational-aid-study/

[3]**tadpole:** a small creature that lives in water and is the young form of a frog
[4]**distract:** to take someone's attention away from what they are trying to do

B. VOCABULARY Here are some words from Reading 2. Read the sentences. Then match each bold word with its definition below.

____ 1. Libraries are using **digital** technology. Many library books are now available as e-books, which people can download onto their computers.

____ 2. Although some parents are **in favor of** tablets in the classroom, other parents complain that children already spend too much time on screens.

____ 3. People can find **reliable** information on websites from professional organizations, but personal websites are less trustworthy.

____ 4. It is a good idea for parents to **monitor** how much time their children spend online because they can easily lose track of time.

____ 5. When my teacher sends me **feedback** on my essay, I read his comments and try to make changes to improve it.

____ 6. Most smartphones have screens that **adapt** to light. When it is dark outside, the screen changes so it is less bright.

____ 7. Apps have **revolutionized** early childhood education. Babies used to learn colors and shapes from books, but now many learn them from apps.

____ 8. The Internet has helped to grow a **global** community of users who communicate and work together from all parts of the world.

____ 9. There are many computer games online that let students review math in fun and **interactive** ways.

____ 10. In college, Sultan **discovered** that he liked art and engineering, so he decided to get a degree in architecture.

6 a. *(v.)* to change because the situation or environment you are in has changed

3 b. *(adj.)* that you can trust

9 c. *(adj.)* involving direct communication both ways, between the computer and the person using it

10 d. *(v.)* to find or learn something new or unexpected

1 e. *(adj.)* using an electronic system to record or store information

7 f. *(v.)* to change something completely

2 g. *(prep. phr.)* supporting and agreeing with something or somebody

5 h. *(n.)* information about something that you have done or made which tells you how good or successful it is

8 i. *(adj.)* covering or affecting the whole world

4 j. *(v.)* to check, record, or watch something regularly for a period of time

iQ PRACTICE Go online for more practice with the vocabulary.
Practice > Unit 3 > Activity 8

Vocabulary words in bold are adjectives? Which are nouns?

C. RESTATE Take notes on the main ideas of each paragraph in Reading 2. Then write the number of the paragraph that each statement summarizes.

_7_ 1. Tablet computers may improve students' scores on reading and math exams.

_5_ 2. Tablets are helping students in the UAE be more creative and learn more.

_8_ 3. Having a poor Internet connection or no Internet can cause problems for students at home.

_3_ 4. Governments are investing in tablet education to prepare students for the future.

_10_ 5. Students, teachers, and parents must all work together to make tablet education successful.

_9_ 6. Some teachers complain that they lose their students' attention because of tablets.

_6_ 7. Tablets allow students to communicate with students from countries around the world.

D. CATEGORIZE Take notes on the supporting details of each paragraph in Reading 2. Then read the statements. Write *T* (true) or *F* (false). Then correct each false statement to make it true according to the article.

_T_ 1. Tablets can be used in history and science classes.

_F_ 2. The Global Book Series is only used by American schoolchildren.

_F_ 3. In the future, most available jobs will be in science and education.

_T_ 4. Students in the UAE use apps to explore and design cities.

_F_ 5. Kristen Wideen is a teacher in Singapore who uses tablets in her classroom.

_F_ 6. Middle school students in California scored 20 percent better on reading tests because of tablets.

_T_ 7. Some students don't benefit from tablets because they don't have Internet at home.

E. IDENTIFY Read these sentences from Reading 2. Then answer the questions. Find the sentences in the reading to help you.

1. (Paragraph 1) When **they** need help, they type a quick message to their teacher, who monitors them from his computer.

   Who does *they* refer to? ___students___

2. (Paragraph 3) **They** want their students to be prepared for the future, where jobs in science and technology will dominate.

   Who does *they* refer to? ___many governments___

3. (Paragraph 4) According to **them**, one of the biggest advantages is tablets allow students to be more creative.

   Who does *them* refer to? _educators_

4. (Paragraph 5) With tablet technology, they can "walk through" **it** as if they were really there.

   What does *it* refer to? _ancient city_ (tablet technology)

5. (Paragraph 6) **They** have a much bigger audience for their ideas.

   Who does *they* refer to? _students_

6. (Paragraph 7) A study of 266 kindergarten students in the United States showed that students with tablets scored higher on every reading test, compared to students without **them**.

   What does *them* refer to? _tablets_

F. **EVALUATE** Read these sentences from Reading 2. Underline the words that show the author's tone (i.e., how the author feels about the topic). Then circle the best description of the tone.

1. They watch them, they hear them, and <u>the places feel much more real than maps ever would</u>.

   (a.) approving   b. disapproving

2. Without tablets, <u>students are limited</u> to communicating with their teacher and the other students in their classroom.

   ✓ a. critical   b. factual

3. Still, no technology is perfect. Many students are often expected to complete tablet assignments at home.

   ✓ a. idealistic best idea   ✓ b. realistic real

4. But, if students, parents, and teachers can work together, the "classroom without walls" could become the classroom of the future and prepare children even better for our connected, digital world.

   a. doubtful   ✓ b. hopeful

G. **COMPOSE** Do you believe tablets should replace books in schools? Write a paragraph of 5–8 sentences giving your opinion.

H. EXTEND Discuss the questions in a group. Look back at your Quick Write on page 63 as you think about what you learned.

1. Some people believe tablets can cause children to become addicted to technology. Do you agree? Why or why not?

2. What job would you like to have in the future? Do you think you will need strong computer and technology skills to perform this job?

WORK WITH THE VIDEO

A. PREVIEW Do computer programs and apps affect your daily life? How? Share your opinion with a partner.

VIDEO VOCABULARY

aspect (n.) one of the qualities, or parts of a situation, idea, problem, etc.

determine: (v.) to make something happen in a particular way

confirm (v.) to say or show that something is true; to make something definite

recover (v.) to return to a normal state after an unpleasant or unusual experience or a period of difficulty

take over (v. phr.) begin to have control of or responsibility for something, especially in the place of somebody else

iQ RESOURCES Go online to watch the video about algorithms.
Resources › Video › Unit 3 › Unit Video

B. IDENTIFY Watch the video two or three times. Then answer the questions.

1. What is an algorithm?

_____

2. Why do credit card companies use algorithms?

_____

3. How are algorithms used by hospitals?

_____

4. How did a computer algorithm affect American markets in 2010?

_____

5. What problem may algorithms cause in the future?

_____

C. EXTEND Do you see ads targeted at you on the social media sites you use? Do you think algorithms such as these can have negative consequences? Write a paragraph of 5–8 sentences in response.

WRITE WHAT YOU THINK

SYNTHESIZE Think about Reading 1, Reading 2, and the unit video as you discuss these questions. Then choose one question and write a paragraph in response.

1. How much control should people have over the technology they use? Why?

2. What positive and negative effects can technology have on people's lives?

VOCABULARY SKILL Synonyms

Synonyms are words that have similar meanings. Learning synonyms will increase your vocabulary and will give your writing more variety.

⌈ People's <u>lifestyles</u> have changed because of new technology.
⌊ People's <u>habits and behaviors</u> have changed because of new technology.

Be careful when choosing synonyms because they do not always have exactly the same meaning. A synonym can have a more general meaning or a more specific meaning.

⌈ **General:** Drivers are expected to <u>follow</u> the rules of the road.
⌊ **Specific:** Drivers are expected to <u>obey</u> the rules of the road.

Follow is more general because it means to do what you are told. *Obey* is more specific because it suggests you *must* do what you are told.

TIP FOR SUCCESS

A **thesaurus** is a book that lists synonyms. Remember that words can have multiple meanings. When you check a thesaurus, make sure you look for the correct synonym for the word.

A. RESTATE Rewrite each sentence by replacing the bold word or phrase with a synonym from the box.

benefits	discover	experiments	occurs
~~data~~	eventually	limitations	

1. The GPS navigation system stores **information** about highway exits and speed limits.

   <u>The GPS navigation system stores data about highway exits and speed limits.</u>

2. When an accident **happens**, the police must decide who is responsible.

   _____ occurs _____

3. Are there any **disadvantages** to using robots for everyday tasks?

   _____ limitations _____

4. Engineers are trying to **find** new ways to increase Internet speeds.

   _____ discover _____

5. Researchers have created **tests** that study how driverless cars respond to accidents.

_____ experiments _____

_____

6. It may be difficult for consumers to accept driverless cars, but **in the end**, they may become popular because they have many **advantages**.   eventually

_____ benefits _____

_____

B. **CATEGORIZE** Read each pair of sentences. Look at the synonyms in bold. Write *G* next to the sentence that uses a more general synonym. Write *S* next to the one that uses a more specific synonym.

1. a. _G_ Driverless cars may give people the **opportunity** to read while driving.

   b. _S_ Driverless cars may give people the **freedom** to read while driving.

2. a. _G_ Sensors can tell the car if an accident **is going to** occur.

   b. _S_ Sensors can tell the car if an accident **is about to** occur.

3. a. _S_ Tablet computers **are revolutionizing** education on a global scale.

   b. _G_ Tablet computers **are changing** education on a global scale.

4. a. _S_ The students must **complete** their homework from home.

   b. _G_ The students must **do** their homework from home.

5. a. _S_ Tablets allow teachers to give students feedback **instantly**.   فورا

   b. _G_ Tablets allow teachers to give students feedback **quickly**.

iQ PRACTICE   Go online for more practice with synonyms.
Practice > Unit 3 > Activity 9

At the end of this unit, you will write a summary paragraph and a personal response paragraph. These paragraphs will include specific information from Reading 2 and your own ideas.

WRITING SKILL Writing a summary and a personal response

A **summary** paragraph tells the reader the main ideas of a reading in your own words. A good summary begins by restating the main idea of the reading. It gives a basic outline of the reading and includes supporting details that are necessary to understand the main points. A summary uses synonyms and similar language to restate ideas from the reading.

A summary is often followed by a **personal response** paragraph. A personal response paragraph gives your personal reaction to the reading. It often includes ideas that you agree or disagree with and gives reasons why you agree or disagree.

A. WRITING MODEL Read the model summary and personal response to Reading 1. Then answer the questions on page 73.

According to the article "Cars That Think," in the near future, driverless cars may change the way people drive. The cars use technology that is already in many modern cars, such as GPS, sensors, and cameras. The sensors see the road and make decisions about turns and stops, and the GPS navigation system tells the car where to go. Car manufacturers say driverless cars are safer and use less gasoline. However, they cannot understand real-life situations, like obeying police instructions, as well as humans can. Also, it is not clear who is at fault when a driverless car causes an accident. The success of these cars will eventually depend on consumers, not car manufacturers.

I was surprised to read about cars that can drive themselves. To me, it sounds like something from a futuristic movie, not real life. I understand why some people would like to own a driverless car, but I don't agree that they are the cars of the future for two reasons. First of all, I personally think that people would prefer to be in control when driving. People know that they are better at reacting to unexpected situations than a machine. They would feel terrible if their driverless car caused an accident that they could have avoided if they were in control. Also, I think people would worry about the car's computer making mistakes. Computers can shut down, get viruses, and have errors. Nobody wants to experience these problems when they drive.

1. Which sentence summarizes the main idea of the reading?

   _____

2. Read these sentences from Reading 1. Write the sentences from the model on page 72 that summarize them.

   a. The sensors can "see" turns, red lights, stop signs, and other cars. Its computer uses GPS and other data to drive the car safely to its destination.

      _____

      _____

   b. In addition, if an accident does occur, who is to blame? Do you blame the driver? The car? The car manufacturer?

      _____

      _____

   c. In the end, consumers will decide if driverless cars are to become the cars of the future.

      _____

      _____

3. Does the writer of the model summary have a positive or negative reaction to driverless cars? How do you know?

   _____

   _____

4. What reasons does the writer give to support his or her opinions?

   _____

   _____

   _____

   _____

5. Do you agree with the writer? Why or why not?

   _____

   _____

   _____

   _____

B. RESTATE Answer the questions to gather ideas for your summary paragraph about Reading 2. Write complete sentences.

1. Why are governments around the world supporting tablet education?

_____

_____

2. Why are teachers in favor of using tablets?

_____

_____

3. How have tablets affected students' test scores?

_____

_____

4. What are some disadvantages of students using tablets?

_____

_____

5. What will students, teachers, and parents need to do to make tablet education successful?

_____

_____

6. How does the author feel about the idea of putting tablets in all schools in the future?

_____

_____

C. EVALUATE Answer the questions to gather ideas for your personal response paragraph about Reading 2. Write complete sentences.

1. What is your personal reaction to using tablets in schools?

_____

_____

2. Is your reaction positive or negative? Why?

_____

_____

3. Do you agree with the author that tablets could better prepare students for future jobs in science and technology? Why or why not?

_____

_____

iQ PRACTICE Go online for more practice with writing summaries and responses. *Practice > Unit 3 > Activity 10*

GRAMMAR Parallel structure

Parallel structure means using the same word form or grammatical structure to list ideas that come in a sequence. Using parallel structure makes your writing clearer and more effective. Use the conjunctions *and, but,* and *or* to connect parallel ideas. Look at the examples of parallel and nonparallel structures.

Parallel: Now students are taking tests *and* quizzes on their tablets.
noun   noun

Not parallel: Now students are taking tests and there are quizzes on their tablets.

Parallel: Machines make our coffee *and* clean our dishes.
verb   verb

Not parallel: Machines make our coffee and our dishes are cleaned.

Parallel: People can tell the car to drive cautiously *or* aggressively.
adv.   adv.

Not parallel: People can tell the car to drive with caution or aggressively.

iQ RESOURCES Go online to watch the Grammar Skill Video.
Resources > Video > Unit 3 > Grammar Skill Video

A. IDENTIFY Read these sentences from the readings. Underline the parallel structures and identify the word forms. Circle the conjunctions.

1. Robots <u>do</u> the vacuuming, <u>mop</u> the floors, (and) <u>mow</u> our yards hands-free.
   verb   verb   verb

2. Sensors built into cars sound an alarm if drivers get too close to a person or another vehicle.

3. They might not recognize when a police officer tells traffic to stop or pull off the road.

4. More schools are using tablets instead of paper or books.

5. Students can also email or text their teachers for help.

6. Other times, Internet connections are slow or stop working.

7. But, if students, parents and teachers can work together, the "classroom without walls" could become the classroom of the future.

B. COMPOSE Combine each pair of sentences into one. Use *and, but,* or *or* and parallel structure.

1. They are not listening to their teacher. They are not taking notes in their science journals.

   They are not listening to their teacher or taking notes in their
   science journals.

2. They turn their designs into a presentation. They share them on their screens.

   _____

   _____

3. After they complete their assignments, some students end up playing a game. Some students end up texting a friend.

   _____

4. Do you blame the driver? Do you blame the car? Do you blame the car manufacturer?

   _____

5. Drivers can make bad judgments. They can get sleepy. They can run red lights.

   _____

6. Driverless cars are already on the roads. They could soon end up at a dealer near you.

   _____

   _____

iQ PRACTICE Go online for more practice with parallel structure.
Practice > Unit 3 > Activities 11–12

UNIT ASSIGNMENT	**Write a summary and a personal response paragraph**
OBJECTIVE ▶	In this assignment, you are going to write two paragraphs. In the first paragraph, you will write a summary of Reading 2. In the second paragraph, you will write your personal response about the use of tablets in the classroom. As you prepare your paragraphs, think about the Unit Question, "How has technology affected our lives?" Use information from Reading 1, Reading 2, the unit video, and your work in this unit to support your paragraphs. Refer to the Self-Assessment checklist on page 78.

iQ PRACTICE Go online to the Writing Tutor to read a model summary and personal response paragraph. *Practice > Unit 3 > Activity 13*

PLAN AND WRITE

A. BRAINSTORM Follows these steps to help you gather your ideas.

1. For your summary paragraph, write the main idea of Reading 2 in your own words.

   Main idea: _____

2. For your personal response paragraph, write your thoughts about schools using tablet-based instruction. Think about these questions as you write:

   • Are there ideas or opinions that you agree or disagree with?

   • Do you think the school tablet experiment will work?

   • Did anything in the reading surprise you?

B. PLAN Follow these steps to plan your paragraphs.

1. For your summary paragraph, look at the sentences you wrote in Activity B on page 74. Circle the details that support the main idea.

iQ RESOURCES Go online to download and complete the outline for your summary paragraph. *Resources > Writing Tools > Unit 3 > Outline*

2. For your personal response paragraph, look at the sentences you wrote in Activity C on page 74.

iQ RESOURCES Go online to download and complete the outline for your personal response paragraph. *Resources > Writing Tools > Unit 3 > Outline*

C. WRITE Use your planning notes to write your paragraph.

1. Write your summary paragraph first. Then write your personal response paragraph.

2. Look at the Self-Assessment checklist below to guide your writing.

iQ PRACTICE Go online to the Writing Tutor to write your assignment.
Practice > Unit 3 > Activity 14

REVISE AND EDIT

iQ RESOURCES Go online to download the peer review worksheet.
Resources > Writing Tools > Unit 3 > Peer Review Worksheet

A. PEER REVIEW Read your partner's paragraphs. Then use the peer review worksheet. Discuss the review with your partner.

B. REWRITE Based on your partner's review, revise and rewrite your paragraphs.

C. EDIT Complete the Self-Assessment checklist as you prepare to write the final draft of your paragraphs. Be prepared to hand in your work or discuss it in class.

SELF-ASSESSMENT	Yes	No
Does the summary paragraph give the main idea of Reading 2 and include supporting details?	☐	☐
Does the personal response paragraph include reasons for the writer's opinion?	☐	☐
Are parallel structures used correctly?	☐	☐
Is there a variety of synonyms used?	☐	☐
Do the paragraphs include vocabulary from the unit?	☐	☐
Did you check the paragraphs for punctuation, spelling, and grammar?	☐	☐

D. REFLECT Discuss these questions with a partner or group.

1. What is something new you learned in this unit?

2. Look back at the Unit Question—How has technology affected our lives? Is your answer different now than when you started the unit? If yes, how is it different? Why?

iQ PRACTICE Go to the online discussion board to discuss the questions.
Practice > Unit 3 > Activity 15

TRACK YOUR SUCCESS

iQ PRACTICE   Go online to check the words and phrases you have learned in this unit. *Practice > Unit 3 > Activity 16*

Check (✓) the skills you learned. If you need more work on a skill, refer to the page(s) in parentheses.

CRITICAL THINKING ☐ I can identify advantages and disadvantages. (p. 61)

READING ☐ I can take notes. (p. 62)

VOCABULARY ☐ I can recognize and use synonyms. (p. 70)

WRITING ☐ I can write a summary and a personal response. (p. 72)

GRAMMAR ☐ I can use parallel structure. (p. 75)

OBJECTIVE ▶ ☐ I can gather information and ideas to write a summary and a personal response paragraph about how technology has affected our lives.

Marketing

4

Does advertising help or harm us?

A. Discuss these questions with your classmates.

1. Have you ever bought something because of an online ad? Do you think you were targeted to receive the ad? Why or why not?

2. Has an advertisement ever helped you in some way? What kind of ad was it? How did it help you?

B. Listen to *The Q Classroom* online. Then answer these questions.

1. Complete the chart with the ideas from the box. Then decide if each student thinks advertising helps or harms us.

It makes us want things we don't need.

~~It gives us information about new products.~~

It pays for a lot of things I like.

You can't trust the information you get from advertising.

	How does advertising help or harm us?	Helps/Harms
Yuna	It gives us information about new products.	helps us
Felix	*are* Polution - no need we buy	
Marcus	buy things you buy - watch free tv show	
Sophy		

Handwritten annotations: "Harm more than help", "help", "not good information"

2. Which student do you agree with the most? Can you think of any examples of how advertising helps or harms us to support your ideas?

iQ PRACTICE Go to the online discussion board to discuss the Unit Question with your classmates. *Practice › Unit 4 › Activity 1*

UNIT OBJECTIVE

Read the articles and gather information and ideas to write an opinion essay on advertising.

READING 1

OBJECTIVE ▶

Can Targeted Ads Change You?

You are going to read an article from a university news site about targeted advertising. Use the article to gather information and ideas for your Unit Assignment.

PREVIEW THE READING

A. PREVIEW Read the title and first paragraph. What is the article's main idea? Check (✓) your answer.

☐ to show how much information advertisers know about you

☐ to show how you might feel differently after getting an ad

☐ to find out how advertisers find information about you

B. QUICK WRITE Do you receive a lot of advertisements online? Do you find the products interesting? How do you think advertisers decide to place their ads? Write for 5–10 minutes in response. Be sure to use this section for your Unit Assignment.

C. VOCABULARY Check (✓) the words you know. Then work with a partner to locate each word in the reading. Use clues to help define the words you don't know. Check your definitions in the dictionary.

accurate *(adj.)* ⚷ OPAL	impact *(n.)* ⚷ OPAL	relevant *(adj.)* ⚷ OPAL
acknowledge *(v.)* ⚷ OPAL	imply *(v.)* ⚷ OPAL	specifically *(adv.)* ⚷ OPAL
factor *(n.)* ⚷ OPAL	reflect *(v.)* ⚷ OPAL	suggest *(v.)* ⚷ OPAL

⚷ Oxford 3000™ words   **OPAL** Oxford Phrasal Academic Lexicon

iQ PRACTICE Go online to listen and practice your pronunciation.
Practice ▸ Unit 4 ▸ Activity 2

WORK WITH THE READING

 A. INVESTIGATE Read the article and gather information about whether advertising helps or harms us.

Home   Sign in

NEW POSTS   ABOUT   SUBSCRIBE

CAN TARGETED ADS CHANGE YOU?

1   Imagine that you're browsing on the Internet and an ad pops up for a jazz concert at a popular club. You're happy that you received the ad, and then another ad appears offering you a coupon for a discount ticket to the jazz concert. You have some interest in jazz music, but now that you have received this ad, you feel differently. Someone else recognized that you are a jazz music enthusiast. You start to believe that about yourself. And you might actually purchase the coupon for the concert.

2   This change in how you see yourself may be the result of receiving an advertisement that was targeted to you **specifically**. When advertisers look at where you go on the Internet, they use algorithms to make a profile of you. Then they use this information about you to find ads for products that you might be interested in. So, the ad is, in a way, designed just for you. It is personalized to your characteristics. This type of ad is called a "behaviorally targeted" ad. A new study suggests that when you receive an ad like this, you might change how you think about yourself.

3   In the study, researchers worked with college students to explore just how behaviorally targeted ads might change how people feel about themselves. In one experiment, participants were asked to plan a weekend trip to Atlanta, Georgia. They were instructed to spend ten minutes researching places to stay, restaurants, and things to do in Atlanta. When they finished, they went on the Internet to browse. This created their "browsing history" for the targeted ad.

4   Then the participants were shown an ad for a sophisticated restaurant. Some of the participants were told that they received the ad because of their browsing history (behaviorally targeted). Others were told that they received the ad because of other **factors**, like their gender or age. And a third group was told nothing at all about why they received the ad. Finally, they all received an ad for a discount coupon for the restaurant. They needed to answer questions about how likely they would be to buy the coupon for the restaurant.

5   The results showed that the participants who had been behaviorally targeted to receive the ad were more likely to purchase the coupon. In fact, they answered questions describing themselves as "sophisticated." They also **acknowledged** that they received the ad because the advertisers **implied** that they were sophisticated. They then saw themselves as sophisticated. The others in the study were less likely to purchase the coupon.

6   In another part of the study, participants chose products from a list of different items, such as laundry detergent or light bulbs. Among the items were environmentally-friendly, or "green" products. Based on their choices, some of the participants then received an ad for another green product. Those who received this ad believed that they were environmentally aware. They purchased the green product and even took it one step further. They donated money to an environmental organization at the end of the study. They perceived themselves as environmentally aware and acted on this characteristic.

7   The results of the study seem to **suggest** that behaviorally targeted ads can have an **impact** on the consumer. However, there are three conditions for the ads to be effective. First, the ad must be based on the consumer's past online behavior. E-3 Second, the consumer must know that he or she is receiving a behaviorally targeted ad. Finally, the ad must be **accurate**. In other words, the ad must **reflect** some interest in the product by the consumer.) E-2

8   In a further test, participants received an ad for hiking boots. Those participants who enjoyed occasional outdoor activities, such as nature walks, expressed interest in the product. After receiving the ad, they thought of themselves as "outdoorsy" and said that they would likely purchase the product. They might even do something related to this characteristic, like go for a hike! For participants with no interest in outdoor activities, the ad had no effect. They did not think differently about themselves, and it did not affect their behavior.

9   What does this mean for the average consumer? With the current technology in advertising, you might receive ads for products that you are interested in. You will know that the ad is related to your past online activity by the blue icon in the corner of the ad. This icon indicates that you are receiving the ad because of your past behavior on the Internet. After receiving this type of ad, you might change how you see yourself. For example, you might become a sophisticated food consumer or an environmentally aware person.

10   And is this so bad? Some people feel that advertisers have too much information about them. They find this to be disturbing, even scary. But others feel differently. Wouldn't you rather receive ads for products or activities that are **relevant** to who you are? You might even find something about yourself that you never knew.

B. VOCABULARY Complete each sentence with the vocabulary from Reading 1. You may need to change the form of some of the words.

6 accurate *(adj.)*	impact *(n.)* 8	relevant *(adj.)* 3
5 acknowledge *(v.)*	imply *(v.)* 9	specifically *(adv.)* 2
7 factor *(n.)*	4 reflect *(v.)*	suggest *(v.)* 1

1. Recent studies on smart watches ___suggest___ that we will never be free from being "wired."

2. Karen received an online ad for running shoes that was _____ designed for her because she is an avid runner and buys a lot of running clothes.

3. Jack's question at the meeting was not _____ to our discussion of low sales; it was completely off topic.

ACADEMIC LANGUAGE

The corpus shows that *based on* is often used in academic writing.
Based on the results . . .
. . . the research was based on . . .

_____ OPAL
Oxford Phrasal Academic Lexicon

4. Sam recommended some articles on the effects of online advertising. These articles _____ his own views, based on the research he has done.

5. Mr. Santana needs to _____ that marketing is not a good profession for him. He needs to find another area that will use his computer skills better.

6. If you plan to study in a financial area such as accounting, you need to make sure that your work is always _____.

7. One _____ that has caused changes in advertising is the popularity of social media.

8. People are constantly on their smartphones; this has had a huge _____ on how people communicate.

9. The students are looking at their phones. This _____ to the instructor that they are not interested in the class.

iQ PRACTICE Go online for more practice with the vocabulary.
Practice › Unit 4 › Activity 3

C. IDENTIFY Read the main ideas. Write the paragraph number where they are found.

_5_ 1. The participants who received the behaviorally targeted ad were more likely to purchase the discount coupon for the sophisticated restaurant.

_7_ 2. Behaviorally targeted ads are only effective if three qualifications are met.

_2_ 3. Advertisers research your browsing history to make ads personally designed for you.

_6_ 4. One experiment showed that people felt more environmentally aware after receiving an ad for a "green" product.

_3_ 5. In the first experiment, participants planned a trip to Atlanta and then browsed the Internet to create a browsing history.

_8_ 6. If you have an interest in outdoor activities, you might show interest in an ad for hiking boots.

D. CATEGORIZE Read the statements. Write _T_ (true) or _F_ (false). Then correct each false statement to make it true according to the article.

_F_ ___ 1. ~~All~~ *Some* of the participants in the first study believed that they had characteristics implied by ads they received.

_T_ ___ 2. Advertisers find information about you from the sites you browse on the Internet.

_F_ ___ 3. Participants who were told they received the ad based on their ~~gender~~ *Past browser history* were more interested in the product.

_T_ ___ 4. Some ads implied that the consumer had particular characteristics, like being sophisticated.

_F_ ___ 5. If consumers know they received an ad because of their past browsing history, they will be ~~less~~ *more* interested in the product.

_F_ ___ 6. An ad sent to a consumer about a product or event that he or she has no interest in will be effective. *with not be effective*

E. IDENTIFY The article mentions three conditions for behaviorally targeted ads to be effective. Look at the conditions in the chart. Then find an example of each from the article. Indicate the paragraph that included the example.

Condition	Example
1. The consumer must know he or she received this ad because of his or her past online behavior.	Para. 4: Some of the participants were told that they received the ad because of their browsing history.
2. The ad must be accurate to the consumer's interest.	_8_ Participants who enjoyed outdoors activities (hiking
3. The ad must be based on the consumer's past online activity.	_6-4_ coupon, browsing history green item based on behavior

F. SYNTHESIZE Look back at your Quick Write on page 82. Can you think of any instances where you have felt happy about receiving an ad? Add any new ideas or information you learned from the reading.

iQ PRACTICE Go online for additional reading and comprehension.
Practice > Unit 4 > Activity 4

WRITE WHAT YOU THINK

A. DISCUSS Discuss the questions in a group. Think about the Unit Question, "Does advertising help or harm us?"

1. Do you find it helpful to receive ads based on your online browsing? Give examples of how such ads might save you time or money.

2. Do you think that advertisers should make a profile of you? Do you think this is an invasion of privacy? Explain your view.

3. Have you received an advertisement for something that is based on a certain characteristic or interest that you have? Did you continue to get more and more ads for products related to this interest? How did you feel about the repeated ads?

B. CREATE Choose one of the questions from Activity A and write a paragraph in response. Look back at your Quick Write on page 82 as you think about what you learned.

READING SKILL Distinguishing facts from opinions

A **fact** is a statement that is true and can be proven true. An **opinion** usually expresses a personal judgment or gives a position about something. Good readers can quickly tell whether a statement is a fact or an opinion. Look at these two statements.

> My parents have been married for 25 years. (fact)
> Relationships with human beings are messy and unpredictable. (opinion)

The first statement is a fact. We can find the date of their marriage and prove it. The second statement is an opinion. It cannot be proven, and people could have a different opinion about relationships from the writer's. In addition, adjectives such as *messy* and *unpredictable* indicate the writer's opinion. Here are two more examples.

> Class starts at 7:30 a.m. (fact)
> My classes are difficult. (opinion)

iQ RESOURCES Go online to watch the Reading Skill Video.
Resources > Video > Unit 4 > Reading Skill Video

verb: feel, belive → opinion

A. CATEGORIZE Read the statements. Write *F* (fact) or *O* (opinion).

F ___ 1. Some ads try to make people aware of social problems.

F ___ 2. There were eight ads for appliances in a recent news magazine.

O ___ 3. Advertising can be ignored easily.

F ___ 4. During every half-hour television show, there are 12 minutes of commercial advertising.

O ___ 5. The ads during the sports program were very funny.

O ___ 6. Ads create a dangerous climate of distrust.

O ___ 7. Online ads make it difficult to read articles.

B. IDENTIFY Read the sentences. Underline the part of each sentence that makes it an opinion.

1. I think people are always influenced by ads.

2. Taken individually, ads are silly, sometimes funny, but certainly nothing to worry about.

3. My favorite ad is the one showing the family in the beautiful new car.

4. That was the most ridiculous ad I have ever seen.

5. The consequences of ads are harmful.

6. I find it creepy that advertisers know so much about me.

iQ PRACTICE Go online for more practice with distinguishing facts from opinions. *Practice > Unit 4 > Activity 5*

In Defense of Advertising

OBJECTIVE ▶

You are going to read an article based on a Canadian radio show. It gives us a less common opinion of advertising. Use the article to gather information and ideas for your Unit Assignment.

PREVIEW THE READING

A. PREVIEW Read the title and first sentence of each paragraph. Do you think the writer finds advertising to be positive or negative? Check (✓) your answer.

☐ positive   ☐ negative

B. QUICK WRITE Think about an advertisement that provided useful information about something important to you. Write for 5–10 minutes in response. Be sure to use this section for your Unit Assignment.

C. VOCABULARY Work with a partner to find the words in the reading. Circle clues in the text that help you understand the meaning of each word. Then use a dictionary to define any unknown words.

annoying *(adj.)* 🔑	donation *(n.)*	memorable *(adj.)*
annual *(adj.)* 🔑 OPAL	entertain *(v.)* 🔑	support *(v.)* 🔑 OPAL
broadcasting *(n.)*	exposure *(n.)*	surrounding *(adj.)* 🔑

🔑 Oxford 3000™ words   **OPAL** Oxford Phrasal Academic Lexicon

iQ PRACTICE Go online to listen and practice your pronunciation.
Practice ▸ Unit 4 ▸ Activity 6

WORK WITH THE READING

🔊 **A. INVESTIGATE** Read the article and gather information about whether advertising helps or harms us.

IN DEFENSE OF 📢 ADVERTISING

1   How often do we hear comments such as these: "I hate advertising," or "There's too much advertising in the world!" In the 21st century, it seems that advertising is everywhere we look. We see it along highways, in trains, buses, even in taxicabs, as well as on the Internet and on TV. It's hard to escape advertising. But do we really want to? Actually, when you think about it, advertising provides us with quite a few benefits.

2   First, advertising gives us information that we need. For instance, if you want to buy a new appliance or a new car, you can look for the best "deals" in ads that appear in newspapers, in magazines, on television, or even on the radio. These ads give you details about the product and help you find out where you can get the best price for something. You don't actually have to go to lots of different stores. So, in this way, advertising provides a service for the consumer.

3   Besides providing information, advertising also **supports** the entertainment industry, including television and radio. It may be **annoying** to sit through commercials during your favorite TV show, but the advertisers have paid for its production. This, in turn, pays the TV crew for their work. Even public **broadcasting** has supporters. The companies' names appear at the beginning or end of the shows. Without their support, there would be more hours of pledge drives[1] asking you, the consumer, for more money. Many presenters, such as newsreaders, get their starts from writing or appearing in commercials or print advertisements. It's a way for them to get both experience and **exposure**.

4   And what about advertising and sports? There are hundreds of large banners **surrounding** sports stadiums, and hundreds, thousands, even millions of people notice them. Professional sports depend on advertising to pay for the fields, the equipment, and yes, even the salaries of professional athletes. Think about the Super Bowl in the United States. Everyone looks forward to this **annual** event, even those who do not like football, because the commercials are known to be the best of the year. Companies pay as much as a million dollars for 60 seconds of advertising time during this event, so a lot of effort

[1] **pledge drive:** an effort by a group of people to raise money, which people promise to pay, for a certain purpose or group

goes into these commercials. As a result, viewers want to watch the commercials almost as much as the sports.

5   When we're not out shopping or being **entertained**, many of us enjoy surfing the Web. Whenever you open a page in Google or access an online newspaper, such as the *New York Times*, there are dozens of ads. These ads help pay for the services that the websites provide. Without the advertising, the websites could not provide those services. They would not have the money to continue.

6   There has always been a "good" side to advertising in the form of public service announcements (PSAs). These are advertisements that provide people with information about issues like diseases or medical problems, as well as public health and safety. The commercials are often very creative and informative. They provide viewers with the information they need in a **memorable** way. Various companies pay for the PSAs, and advertising agencies make **donations** of their time and expertise to produce them.

7   It would be a much duller, certainly less colorful world without advertising. Think of all of the ways that advertising improves our world. The next time you look at that clothing catalog, think of all of the creativity and work that went into making it. From clothing designers and photographers to paper company workers and store employees— thousands of people worked to help produce that catalog. And when you watch your favorite TV show, remember that the commercials were partly responsible for what you've just watched and enjoyed. We may wish that commercials and advertisements weren't necessary, but, for the most part, we are all content to have them as part of our lives.

VOCABULARY SKILL REVIEW

Knowing the part of speech of a vocabulary word can help you understand the text better. Use the context to guess the part of speech of the words in Activity B.

B. VOCABULARY Here are some words from Reading 2. Read the sentences. Then write each bold word next to the correct definition on page 92.

1. Some food companies use part of their profits to **support** programs for seriously ill children.

2. This is a useful website, but I can't stand all of the pop-up ads. They're so **annoying**!

3. Radio **broadcasting** brings news and other programs to the public.

4. The professor's appearance on the news program gave him the **exposure** he needed to become well known.

5. All of the ads on the fence **surrounding** the baseball field are for food products that are sold there.

6. There is always a guest speaker at the college's **annual** graduation dinner. This year it will be the mayor!

7. The children were bored last night, so we turned on the TV to **entertain** them.

8. That was a very **memorable** book. After all these years, I still remember the ending very clearly.

9. Many food companies make a **donation** of their products to organizations that feed the hungry.

a. _____ (adj.) being or going around someone or something 5

b. _____ (v.) to interest and amuse someone 7

c. _____ (n.) attention from newspapers, television, 4 تستلفت الأنظار
or other media

d. _____ (n.) sound or pictures that are sent by radio or television 3

e. _____ (n.) money or something that is given to an organization 9

f. _____ (adj.) happening or done once a year 6

g. _____ (v.) to give or provide someone or something with 1
assistance and money

h. _____ (adj.) making you feel slightly angry 2

i. _____ (adj.) easy to remember because it is special in 8
some way

iQ PRACTICE Go online for more practice with the vocabulary.
Practice > Unit 4 > Activity 7

 ### CRITICAL THINKING STRATEGY

Using a Venn diagram

Using a **Venn diagram** is one way to compare items. A Venn diagram helps
you to see similarities and differences between things. For example, you can
compare the purposes of different kinds of advertisements:

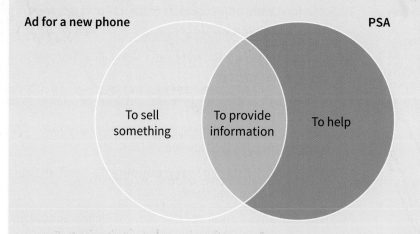

Ad for a new phone   **PSA**

To sell something | To provide information | To help

iQ PRACTICE Go online to watch the Critical Thinking Video and check
your comprehension. *Practice > Unit 4 > Activity 8*

C. ANALYZE Look at the Venn diagram. Complete the diagram using the ideas from the box. Explain your answer choices.

~~can change channels during ads~~
pop up when you don't expect it *online–TV*
targeted ads are just what you want to see *on*
tell stories that you can relate to *on*
create interest in a product without invading privacy *TV–on*
are small; don't take up the whole screen *on*

can be annoying *TV – on*
interrupt what you're watching *on – TV*
interrupt what you're reading *on*
can be fun to watch *TV–on*
can click them off *on < TV*
~~can be funny~~

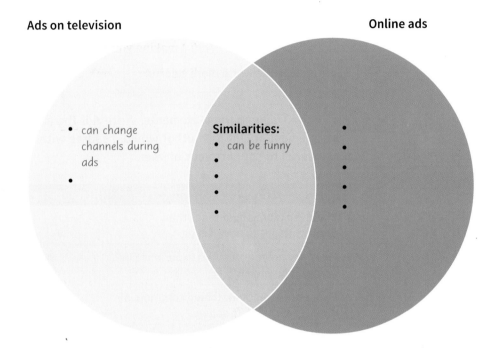

Ads on television

Online ads

• can change channels during ads

•

Similarities:
• can be funny
•
•
•
•

•
•
•
•
•

D. IDENTIFY Read the sentences. Then number them in the order that the ideas appear in the article.

___6___ 1. PSAs provide people with information about things like medical problems.

___4___ 2. Professional sports depend on advertising.

___3___ 3. Advertising helps support broadcasting.

___2___ 4. Ads provide us with helpful information about products we want to buy.

___7___ 5. Advertisements make the world more colorful.

___5___ 6. Ads help pay for the services that websites provide.

E. IDENTIFY Write an example for each of the benefits of advertising listed in the chart.

Benefit	Example
1. provides information for buying something	best deal for new car in newspaper
2. supports broadcasting	*to make their budget*
3. helps support sports	*to pay athlitics*
4. provides public service announcements	*medical issuse*
5. helps make the world more colorful	*everywhere Potograph design*

F. EVALUATE Read the statements. Write *A* if the author would agree with a statement or *D* if the author would disagree with it. Write the paragraph number(s) to support your answer.

	Agree/Disagree	Paragraph #
1. There are more advantages than disadvantages to advertising.	A	1, 7
2. Many newsreaders gained experience by doing commercials.	*A*	*3*
3. Most people enjoy watching commercials during their favorite shows.	*D*	*7 - 1 - 3*
4. Professional sports fields should not have advertising.	*D*	*4*
5. We should have less advertising and more fundraising on TV.	*D*	*3*

G. APPLY Answer the questions. Write the paragraph number where the answer is found. Then discuss your answers with a partner.

1. In professional sports, what are some examples of things that advertising pays for? Paragraph: *4*

   to pay for field, equipment, and salaries of professiona athletes

2. What kinds of professionals work on a clothing catalog? Name at least three. Paragraph: *7*

   designers, photographers and store employees

3. Why is it important that PSAs be very creative? Paragraph: *6*

   They provid viewers with the information they need in a memorable day

4. What would not exist on the Internet if there were no advertising?

Paragraph: _5_

we can't access online newspappers and other services those the Web Provide for us

H. DISCUSS Discuss the questions in a group. Look back at your Quick Write on page 89 as you think about what you learned.

1. Some people say that advertising is a "necessary evil." What does this mean? Do you agree? Why or why not? (If something is *evil*, it is very bad.)

2. Would you be willing to pay more for things and have no advertising?

WORK WITH THE VIDEO

A. PREVIEW Do you know how advertisements sometimes appear on your Facebook page? How do advertisers get information about you? Give examples if you can.

VIDEO VOCABULARY

hoard (v.) to collect and store large quantities of something (often in secrecy)

turn into (v.) (to cause) to become

reveal (v.) to make something known that was previously secret or unknown

monetize (v.) to convert into a form of currency

device (n.) a tool or piece of equipment made for a particular purpose, esp. a piece of mechanical or electronic equipment

innovation (n.) something new that has been introduced

unique (adj.) unlike anything else; being the only one of its type

iQ RESOURCES Go online to watch the video about how tech companies make money from your personal data. *Resources > Video > Unit 4 > Unit Video*

B. CATEGORIZE Watch the video two or three times. Then take notes in the chart.

	Ways advertisers get data	How advertisers use data
Notes from the video	*Facebook can tell advertiser this is th real Person and facebook give ourdata to companies for advertising*	*Companies take our data and join to facbook to find us for advertising*

C. DISCUSS Discuss the questions in a group. If you had to describe the "unique you," which adjectives would you use? How do you think advertisers might describe you? Do you think it is a good or bad thing that advertisers can know so much about you?

WRITE WHAT YOU THINK

SYNTHESIZE Think about Reading 1, Reading 2, and the unit video as you discuss these questions. Then choose one question and write a paragraph in response.

1. Think of an advertisement that you've seen recently that affected you. What was it selling? How did it affect you? Was it positive or negative?

2. Do you think there is too much advertising? Where would you like to see less or no advertising?

3. Did you ever receive a targeted ad? Why do you think you received it? Was it for something you are interested in?

VOCABULARY SKILL Suffixes

A **suffix** is a group of letters that comes at the end of a word, such as *-ful* in *painful*. When you add a suffix to a word, it changes the part of speech. Being familiar with suffixes can help increase your vocabulary. Here is a list of suffixes.

Adjective		Noun		Adverb
-ful	-ial	-ment	-ship	-ly
-able	-er	-tion	-ness	

APPLY Decide which part of speech each word is based on its suffix. Then check (✓) the correct column.

	Adjective	Noun	Adverb
1. unpredictable	✓	☐	☐
2. relationship	☐	✓	☐
3. recently	☐	☐	✓
4. painful	✓	☐	☐
5. dissatisfaction	☐	✓	☐
6. distrustful	✓	☐	☐
7. happiness	☐	✓	☐
8. donation	☐	✓	☐
9. certainly	☐	☐	✓
10. colorful	✓	☐	☐

iQ PRACTICE Go online for more practice with suffixes.
Practice > Unit 4 > Activity 9

WRITING

OBJECTIVE ▶   At the end of this unit, you will write an opinion essay about advertis
This essay will include specific information from the readings, the un
and your own ideas.

WRITING SKILL Writing an opinion essay

In Unit 1, you learned the components, or parts, of a good paragraph. An **essay** is a longer piece of writing, and it has components similar to the ones in a paragraph. In an essay, the first paragraph is the **introductory paragraph**. In an **opinion essay**, the introductory paragraph describes a situation and includes your opinion of it, which is the main idea of the essay. In an essay, this main idea is the **thesis statement**. The thesis statement of an opinion essay clearly expresses how you feel about the topic.

The next paragraphs in an essay are the **body paragraphs**. The body paragraphs support the thesis statement. In an opinion essay, each body paragraph gives a specific reason for your opinion and examples to make it a strong argument. Finally, the **concluding paragraph** is the last paragraph. It restates your opinion, summarizes your reasons for it, and often gives a prediction about it.

A. WRITING MODEL Read the model opinion essay. Then answer the questions on page 98.

introductory
paragraph

Most people love watching some kind of television, but hate the commercials that interrupt the TV programs. I guess you could say that I'm different from most people because I love commercials. In fact, I think the commercials are almost as good as the shows I'm watching. You won't find me leaving the room to get a snack or something to drink when a commercial comes on. I'm the one paying attention because I think television commercials are great!

body paragraph

First of all, I think a lot of commercials are funny. Some advertisers like to make fun of mistakes that people make. For example, a car insurance company has an ad showing a man trimming a tree in his yard. The next thing you know, a huge tree limb falls on his neighbor's car. It's what they used to call slapstick humor, and I think it's very funny. In another example, some guys are moving into a new apartment, and they are installing an air conditioner into a window. It falls out and onto someone's car. I enjoy these kinds of commercials because they provide a glimpse of human behavior that I find entertaining.

body
paragraphs

concluding
paragraph

Additionally, I like to see commercials that my senses respond to, in particular, my sense of taste. When I see a close-up of some mouth-watering food, I get so hungry that I have to eat it. I frequently call for takeout right then and there, or I run to the kitchen and try to create what I've just seen on the screen. When I see a new car ad where the car is driving through mountain roads, it makes me want to book a trip out west to enjoy the same scenery. And when I hear music I like as the background in an ad, I search online to find out the name of the musician so I can listen to that person again.

Finally, TV advertising provides me with information about coming attractions: future TV programs, events, or movies. When I see a commercial for a movie that will soon be released, I can decide if it's something I want to see or not. If there's a TV program coming up, I can set my DVR for it well in advance.

You could say I'm very unusual because I don't mind commercials while I'm watching my favorite TV programs. I don't find commercials to be interruptions. I love them because I think they're funny, entertaining, and informative. I think TV would be pretty dull without them.

1. What is the thesis statement? Underline the thesis statement in the introductory paragraph.

2. What are the three reasons and examples that the writer uses to support his or her opinion?

   Reason 1: _I think a lot of commercials are funny._

   Examples: _A huge tree limb falls on a neighbor's car; an air conditioner_ _falls out a window and onto someone's car._

   Reason 2: _____

   Examples: _____

   _____

   Reason 3: _____

   Examples: _____

   _____

B. EVALUATE Read the introductory paragraphs to different opinion essays. Which is the best thesis statement for each essay? Choose from the statements on page 99.

1. Advertising has been around for many years, and most people just accept it as part of our lives. But I was watching TV with my young son the other night when he pointed out to me the name of a particular computer that he noticed

WRITING TIP
The thesis statement of an essay is similar to the topic sentence of a paragraph. It contains the writer's main idea, position, or opinion. It helps the reader understand the writer's main idea.

on the show we were watching. That's when I realized that advertising has invaded our lives too much. If my son recognizes a company logo that easily, I wonder how much more advertising he is being exposed to without even realizing it? Enough is enough.

a. There should not be any advertising on the Internet.

b. Advertising products within television shows should be banned.

c. We need to find a way to reduce the amount of advertising in our lives.

2. While watching my son's baseball game the other night, I noticed something new on the fence surrounding the field. There was a huge advertisement for a popular brand of soda. I was absolutely shocked! How could an advertisement for junk food be placed in view of all of the children and parents? I realize now that this huge corporation is giving money to my son's school, but at what cost?

a. Advertisements for unhealthy food or drinks should not be on school property.

b. I think soda advertisements are very funny.

c. I think it's wonderful that companies are paying for sports programs.

3. With new technology, advertising can be very deceptive. For example, many beauty ads show women with perfect skin and hair. In reality, their photos have been "touched up" by computer software programs. Men, too, are shown as very muscular and strong, when the reality may be quite different. Men and women both age naturally, but advertisements show a different kind of person—one who never gets old.

a. I think changing the way someone looks in a photo is an outdated advertising trick.

b. I think advertisements should show people of different ages, shapes, and sizes, not just young people.

c. I think computer software programs are very innovative.

4. I was watching TV last night and I realized something about my life: I'm missing a lot of things. When I saw a commercial for a new sports car, I realized I don't have the most modern car. An ad for flat-screen TVs reminded me that my television is eight years old. And finally, the travel commercials reminded me that I don't have the money to travel to exotic places and stay in world-famous resorts. So, in the end, all of these ads make me feel like a failure. This is not why I watch TV.

a. Advertising on TV should provide us with details about all the latest products.

b. Advertising on TV should entertain us.

c. Advertising on TV should not make us feel like we are unsuccessful.

iQ PRACTICE Go online for more practice with writing an opinion essay.
Practice > Unit 4 > Activity 10

A **simple sentence** contains a *subject* and a *verb* and expresses a complete thought or idea. A simple sentence is sometimes called an *independent clause*.

Ahmed drives to work every day.
subject verb

A **compound sentence** contains two **independent clauses** (or simple sentences) joined by a **coordinating conjunction** (*and, but, so, or*). A comma usually comes before the coordinating conjunction in a compound sentence.

Use *and* to combine two sentences with related ideas.

The ad was funny, **and** it gave us helpful information.

Use *but* to combine two sentences with contrasting ideas.

I enjoyed the book, **but** it had a very sad ending.

Use *so* when the second sentence is a result of the first sentence.

Ali isn't feeling well, **so** he isn't coming to class today.

Use *or* when there is a choice or two possibilities.

You can take the train to Madrid, **or** you can fly.

Using different types of sentences can help make your writing more interesting for your reader.

A. APPLY Complete each sentence with *and, but, so,* or *or*. Then write the reason you chose that conjunction (*related ideas, contrasting ideas, a result,* or *a choice*).

1. I am the mother of young children, __and__ I feel that all advertising during children's programming should be banned.

   Reason: __related ideas__

2. The TV advertisement was about a very serious social topic, _____ there were some funny moments in it.

   Reason: _____

3. Children are exposed to many advertisements for unhealthy foods, _____ parents have to educate their children about good food and nutrition.

   Reason: _____

4. Many people think advertisements are harmful, _____ sometimes they can be very helpful.

   Reason: _____

5. We can use a Web ad, _____ we can create a TV ad.

   Reason: _____

B. COMPOSE Combine the sentences with *and, but, so,* or *or.* Add commas.

1. I like to stay healthy. I exercise every day.

   _____

2. Sara Marcone is a very creative writer. She has written five novels.

   _____

3. The lecture was interesting. It was a bit too long.

   _____

4. We can go out for dinner. We can stay home.

   _____

C. COMPOSE Write five compound sentences. Use each conjunction (*and, but, so, or*) at least once.

D. IDENTIFY Find five compound sentences in Reading 2. Underline the sentences and circle the coordinating conjunctions.

iQ PRACTICE Go online for more practice with compound sentences. *Practice > Unit 4 > Activities 11–12*

UNIT ASSIGNMENT Write an opinion essay

OBJECTIVE ▶

In this assignment, you are going to write a four-paragraph opinion essay about advertising. As you prepare your essay, think about the Unit Question, "Does advertising help or harm us?" Use information from Reading 1, Reading 2, the unit video, and your work in this unit to support your essay. Refer to the Self-Assessment checklist on page 102.

iQ PRACTICE Go online to the Writing Tutor to read a model opinion essay. *Practice > Unit 4 > Activity 13*

PLAN AND WRITE

A. BRAINSTORM Think about your answer to the Unit Question, "Does advertising help or harm us?" Then write a list of reasons and examples for your answer or opinion.

B. PLAN Follow these steps to plan your opinion essay.

1. Read your list from Activity A. Circle your best reasons and examples.

2. Write your thesis statement. It should tell the reader your opinion about the topic.

iQ RESOURCES Go online to download and complete the outline for your opinion essay. *Resources > Writing Tools > Unit 4 > Outline*

C. WRITE Use your planning notes to write your essay.

1. Write your opinion essay. Remember to state your opinion in the introductory paragraph. Include at least two reasons for your opinion in the two body paragraphs.

2. Look at the Self-Assessment checklist below to guide your writing.

iQ PRACTICE Go online to the Writing Tutor to write your assignment. *Practice > Unit 4 > Activity 14*

REVISE AND EDIT

iQ RESOURCES Go online to download the peer review worksheet. *Resources > Writing Tools > Unit 4 > Peer Review Worksheet*

A. PEER REVIEW Read your partner's essay. Then use the peer review worksheet. Discuss the review with your partner.

B. REWRITE Based on your partner's review, revise and rewrite your essay.

C. EDIT Complete the Self-Assessment checklist as you prepare to write the final draft of your essay. Be prepared to hand in your work or discuss it in class.

SELF-ASSESSMENT	Yes	No
Does the essay include an introductory paragraph, two body paragraphs, and a concluding paragraph?	☐	☐
Are compound sentences used appropriately?	☐	☐
If words with suffixes are used, are they correct?	☐	☐
Does the essay include vocabulary from the unit?	☐	☐
Did you check the essay for punctuation, spelling, and grammar?	☐	☐

D. REFLECT Discuss these questions with a partner or group.

1. What is something new you learned in this unit?

2. Look back at the Unit Question—Does advertising help or harm us? Is your answer different now than when you started the unit? If yes, how is it different? Why?

iQ PRACTICE Go to the online discussion board to discuss the questions. *Practice > Unit 4 > Activity 15*

TRACK YOUR SUCCESS

iQ PRACTICE Go online to check the words and phrases you have learned in this unit. *Practice > Unit 4 > Activity 16*

Check (✓) the skills you learned. If you need more work on a skill, refer to the page(s) in parentheses.

READING ☐ I can distinguish facts from opinions. (p. 87)

CRITICAL THINKING ☐ I can use a Venn diagram. (p. 92)

VOCABULARY ☐ I can use suffixes. (p. 96)

WRITING ☐ I can write an opinion essay. (p. 97)

GRAMMAR ☐ I can use compound sentences. (p. 100)

OBJECTIVE ▶ ☐ I can gather information and ideas to write an opinion essay on advertising.

Psychology

5

CRITICAL THINKING	justifying your opinion of a text
READING	using referents to understand contrast
VOCABULARY	using the dictionary to find the correct meaning
WRITING	writing a narrative essay
GRAMMAR	shifts between past and present time frames

UNIT QUESTION

How do people overcome obstacles?

A. Discuss these questions with your classmates.

1. What is an obstacle? Describe different types of obstacles that can occur.

2. Do you know someone who overcame an obstacle? What kind of obstacle was it?

3. Look at the photo. What kinds of challenges does the man have? What qualities or characteristics do you think might help him?

B. Listen to *The Q Classroom* online. Then answer these questions.

1. Sophy thinks that it's important to have someone to support you. Why do you think that's important for overcoming obstacles or challenges in your life? Give examples of people who could help someone overcome obstacles.

2. Felix thinks that there are characteristics that a person has that will help him or her overcome challenges. Do you agree with that? What qualities do you think will help you face difficulties in your life?

iQ PRACTICE Go to the online discussion board to discuss the Unit Question with your classmates. *Practice > Unit 5 > Activity 1*

UNIT OBJECTIVE

Read the article and book excerpt and gather information and ideas to write a narrative essay about an obstacle that you've faced.

READING 1

OBJECTIVE ▶

How People Learn to Become Resilient

You are going to read an article from the *New Yorker* about resilience. *Resilience* means being strong enough to recover quickly from damage, an illness, a shock, or change. The article discusses research into how some people are resilient. Use the article to gather information and ideas for your Unit Assignment.

PREVIEW THE READING

A. PREVIEW Read the title and first paragraph. How would you describe the boy in the article? Check (✓) your answers.

- ☐ He has a good home life.
- ☐ He's a happy person.
- ☐ He's unlucky.
- ☐ He feels sorry for himself.
- ☐ He makes the most of his situation.

B. QUICK WRITE Think about an obstacle or challenge that you've overcome. Write for 5–10 minutes in response. Remember to use this section for your Unit Assignment.

C. VOCABULARY Check (✓) the words you know. Then work with a partner to locate each word in the reading. Use clues to help define the words you don't know. Check your definitions in the dictionary.

element *(n.)* 🔑 OPAL	poverty *(n.)* 🔑 OPAL	trait *(n.)*
emerge *(v.)* 🔑 OPAL	predict *(v.)* 🔑 OPAL	traumatic *(adj.)*
enable *(v.)* 🔑 OPAL	set apart *(v. phr.)*	
perceive *(v.)* OPAL	threat *(n.)* 🔑 OPAL	

🔑 Oxford 3000™ words   **OPAL** Oxford Phrasal Academic Lexicon

iQ PRACTICE Go online to listen and practice your pronunciation.
Practice > Unit 5 > Activity 2

WORK WITH THE READING

A. INVESTIGATE Read the article and gather information about how people overcome obstacles.

How People Learn to Become Resilient

By Maria Konnikova

1   Norman Garmezy, a psychologist at the University of Minnesota, met thousands of children in his four decades of research. But one boy in particular stuck with him. He was nine years old, with an ill mother and an absent father. Each day, he would arrive at school with the exact same sandwich: two slices of bread with nothing in between. At home, there was no other food available and no one to make any. Even so, Garmezy would later recall, the boy wanted to make sure that "no one would feel pity for him." Each day, without fail, he would walk in with a smile on his face and a "bread sandwich" tucked into his bag.

2   The boy with the bread sandwich was part of a special group of children. Garmezy identified this group of kids as succeeding, even excelling, despite incredibly difficult circumstances. These were the children who exhibited a **trait** Garmezy would later identify as "resilience."

3   Resilience presents a challenge for psychologists. Finding out if you have it or not largely depends on the way your life unfolds. If you are lucky enough to never experience any sort of adversity, we won't know how resilient you are. It's only when you're faced with obstacles, stress, and other environmental **threats** that resilience, or the lack of it, **emerges**: do you fall apart or do you rise above it?

4   Environmental threats can come in various ways. Some are continuous, such as **poverty** and challenging home conditions. Other threats are acute: experiencing or witnessing a **traumatic** violent encounter, for example, or being in an accident. What matters is the intensity and the duration of the stressful event.

5   Garmezy's work looked at protective factors: the **elements** of an individual's background or personality that could **enable** success despite the challenges the person faced. His research

identified elements that fell into two groups: individual psychological factors and external environmental factors.

6 In 1989, a psychologist named Emmy Werner published the results of a 32-year project. She had followed a group of 698 children in Kauai, Hawaii, from before birth through their third decade of life. Along the way, she'd monitored them for any exposure to stress: poverty, problems in the family, and so on. Two-thirds of the children came from backgrounds that were essentially stable, successful, and happy; the other third qualified as "at risk." Like Garmezy, she soon discovered that not all of the at-risk children reacted to stress in the same way. Two-thirds of them "developed serious learning or behavior problems by the age of ten," or had other more serious mental health and behavior problems as they became older. But the remaining third developed into "competent, confident, and caring young adults." They had attained academic, domestic, and social success—and they were always ready to take advantage of new opportunities that arose.

7 What was it that **set** the resilient children **apart**? She found that several elements **predicted** resilience. Some elements had to do with luck: a resilient child might have a strong bond with a supportive caregiver, parent, teacher, or other mentor-like figure. But another, quite large set of elements was psychological and had to do with how the children responded to the environment. From a young age, resilient children tended to "meet the world on their own terms." They were autonomous and *independent* independent, would seek out new experiences, and had a "positive social orientation." Werner wrote, "Though not especially gifted, these children used whatever skills they had effectively." Perhaps most importantly, the resilient children believed that they, and not their circumstances, affected their achievements. The resilient children saw themselves as being able to make good decisions about their obstacles to improve their future.

8 George Bonanno is a clinical psychologist at Columbia University's Teachers College and has been studying resilience for nearly 25 years. Garmezy, Werner, and others have shown that some people are far better than others at dealing with adversity. Bonanno has been trying to figure out where that variation might come from. One of the central elements of resilience, Bonanno has found, is perception: Do you **perceive** an event as traumatic or as an opportunity to learn and grow? "Events are not traumatic until we experience them as traumatic," Bonanno told me. Take something as terrible as the surprising death of a close friend: you might be sad, but if you can find a way to see that event as filled with meaning—perhaps it leads to greater awareness of a certain disease or to closer ties with the community—then it may not be seen as a trauma. The good news is that positive interpretation can be taught. "We can make ourselves more or less vulnerable by how we think about things," Bonanno said.

B. VOCABULARY Here are some words from Reading 1. Read the se~
Then match each bold word with its definition below.

_g_ 1. The teacher **predicted** that the students would do well on the
achievement test if they continued to do all of their assignments.

_d_ 2. There are many **elements** involved in being a successful student, such as
determination and hard work.

_c_ 3. Even though he grew up in **poverty**, he was able to succeed in life by
working hard and focusing on his education.

_j_ 4. Many people go through **traumatic** events as children, such as the death
of a parent.

_i_ 5. When someone has an experience in a different country, it **sets** them
apart from others who never left their homeland.

_f_ 6. Receiving a seeing-eye dog **enabled** the blind woman to travel to places
on her own.

_b_ 7. Olivia **emerged** as a very competent and confident young woman even
though she was very shy as a child.

_h_ 8. The **threat** of losing his job was a constant fear in his life after he received
a poor evaluation from his boss.

_e_ 9. Some people **perceive** a challenge as stressful, while others see it as a
new opportunity for personal growth.

_a_ 10. One **trait** that resilient people share is that they feel that they are in
control of their lives.

a. *(n.)* a quality or part of someone's character   10

b. *(v.)* to appear or come from somewhere unexpectedly   9

c. *(n.)* the state of having very little money or of being poor

d. *(n.)* an important part of something   2

e. *(v.)* to see or think of something in a particular way   1

f. *(v.)* to make someone able to do something   6

g. *(v.)* to say that something will happen

h. *(n.)* something that indicates future danger   8

i. *(v. phr.)* to make something different from or better than others   5

j. *(adj.)* causing someone to feel great unhappiness or shock   4

iQ PRACTICE Go online for more practice with the vocabulary.
Practice > Unit 5 > Activity 3

CRITICAL THINKING STRATEGY

Justifying your opinion of a text

As readers, we often form opinions about the ideas or statements made in an article. Do we agree with a statement? Does it seem true based on our experience? Good writers support their statements with evidence, for example, from research or from facts and statistics. Before you decide if you agree or disagree with an idea in a text, think about the evidence the writer has provided. Does the evidence **justify your opinion**? Can you give reasons and examples for or against the statements made in the text? You can use knowledge and personal experience to help form your opinion and make it stronger with information from your own research, for example, from reading more articles on the same topic. You can ask:

> *Is the statement supported by evidence?* (Find the evidence in the text.)
>
> *What kind of evidence is it?* (e.g., research, facts, statistics)
>
> *The text quotes a study: Was it a good study?* (e.g., involved lots of people, collected lots of data)
>
> *Do other studies support the idea?* (Do online research.)

Use this information to decide if you agree with the ideas in a text and to justify your opinion in discussions or essays on the topic.

iQ PRACTICE Go online to watch the Critical Thinking Video and check your comprehension. *Practice > Unit 5 > Activity 4*

C. IDENTIFY Read the ideas below. Find the evidence in the text for each idea. Then decide if you agree or disagree.

Idea in text	Agree/Disagree?	Ways to justify opinion
1. Only certain people going through difficult challenges have a quality called *resilience*.	agree	good evidence in text: very long study (32 years) with lots of people (698) check online for more studies
2. There are many factors that predict a person's resilience.	agreed	6-7(P9)
3. The way people perceive events affects their resilience.		8(P)
4. Positive perceptions can be taught.		

D. EXTEND Work with a partner. How can you justify your opinion of the statements? Use the information in the chart and your own ideas. Think of as many ways as you can.

E. CATEGORIZE Read the statements. Write *T* (true) or *F* (false). Then correct each false statement to make it true according to the article.

F _ 1. The boy who Norman Garmezy describes came to school every day with a cheese sandwich and a smile on his face.

T _ 2. When you are resilient, you rise above a situation that is stressful.

F _ 3. An example of a continuous threat, according to Garmezy, is being in an accident.

F _ 4. Emmy Werner found in her study of 698 children that they all reacted to stress in the same way.

T _ 5. One-third of the children Werner studied became successful adults.

F _ 6. According to Werner, the resilient children believed that their life circumstances affected how successful they would be.

T _ 7. George Bonanno believes that the key to resilience is how you perceive an event.

F. IDENTIFY Complete the statements with information from the reading. Then write the paragraph number where the answer is found.

1. Some people belong to a group that succeeds even though they live in _incredebly diff_. Paragraph ___

2. Environmental threats can be either continuous or ___ *aqute*. Paragraph ___

3. Emmy Werner studied children for more than ___ *32* ___ years. Paragraph ___

4. Two-thirds of the children she studied came from ___ *essentially* ___ homes. Paragraph ___

5. Of the "at risk" children that Werner studied, two-thirds of these children had _developed mental_ ___ as they became older. Paragraph ___

6. Werner found that the resilient children had an element of luck, which she described as a bond with _____. Paragraph ___

7. Werner described these resilient children as ___ *attonemes and independent* Paragraph ___

8. Bonanno also feels that positive interpretation of events is something that we can ___ *learned* ___. Paragraph ___

G. IDENTIFY Read the statements. Identify which researcher discovered this information. Write the letter of the researcher. There may be more than one answer.

G (Norman Garmezy)	W (Emmy Werner)	B (George Bonanno)

_G_ 1. How long and how intense a threat is to someone will affect how resilient they are.

_b_ 2. A stressful event will only be traumatic if we perceive it that way.

Gwb 3. There are always some people who respond in a positive way to traumatic events.

_W_ 4. Two-thirds of the children who grew up in very bad situations developed serious behavior problems.

_W_ 5. Resilient people take control of their obstacles by making good decisions, rather than letting their circumstances control them.

_gw_ 6. There are certain factors in one's personality or environment that can help them to deal with stress.

H. EXPAND Look back at your Quick Write on page 106. How do you think you overcame the obstacle? Was it because someone helped you? Or was it the way you perceived the challenge that helped you to deal with it. Or is it a characteristic in your personality that helped you? Add any new ideas or information you learned from the reading.

iQ PRACTICE Go online for additional reading and comprehension.
Practice > Unit 5 > Activity 5

WRITE WHAT YOU THINK

A. DISCUSS Discuss the questions in a group. Think about "How do people overcome obstacles?"

1. Do you see yourself as resilient? Are there certain factors that can e... resilient you are? Do you think that your resilience depends on how seri... challenge is?

2. Look back at the photo on page 108. How do you think the man was able to deal with losing his home? What type of person do you think does the best in dealing with an obstacle like this?

3. Some people see a glass as half full, while others see it as half empty. What does this mean about the perception of the water in the glass? Do you perceive difficulties in a positive way?

B. CREATE Choose one of the questions from Activity A and write a paragraph in response. Look back at your Quick Write on page 106 as you think about what you learned.

READING SKILL Using referents to understand contrast

A **referent** is a word or group of words that refers to a noun that was mentioned previously. Understanding referents will help you become a better reader. In Reading 1, the writer is focusing on what makes one group of people more resilient than others. The writer uses certain words and phrases to refer to this particular group and to the factors leading to resilience throughout the reading.

Words like *this* and *these* refer back to the noun being focused on.

> The boy with the bread sandwich was part of a special group of children. These children stood out from others in similar situations. Garmezy identified this group of kids as succeeding . . .

Words like *some* and *other* show differences among groups of things but still refer back to the noun being focused on.

> Environmental threats can come in various ways. Some are continuous . . . Other threats are acute . . .

> She found that several elements predicted resilience. Some elements had to do with luck . . . But another, quite large set of elements was psychological.

A. IDENTIFY Read the sentences and look at the words in bold. Circle the noun that they refer to.

1. Many children face obstacles growing up, but **some** children seem to deal with **these** problems better than **others**. _(children)_

2. The resilient children displayed a certain kind of personality. **These** children felt they were in control of their life circumstances. Other children felt that their circumstance would never improve.

3. The researchers discovered that there are several elements that help someone be resilient. **Some** of the elements are environmental. **Others** are psychological.

4. Resilient people tend to look at adversity differently. **These** people see obstacles as opportunities for growth. Others tend to feel overwhelmed by life's challenges.

5. Resilience is something that can be taught. **This** quality can develop when we perceive problems differently.

ACADEMIC LANGUAGE
The phrase *tend to* is often used in academic writing. It is more appropriate in an academic context than *usually*.

_____ OPAL
Oxford Phrasal Academic Lexicon

B. RECOGNIZE Read the paragraph about resilient people. Underline the words and phrases that refer to resilient people. Circle the words and phrases that refer to other types of people.

   Some people see the glass as half full, and others see it as half empty. The first group has a trait we call resilience. When adversity strikes, this group of people tends to look at the problem in a positive light. For example, say you lose your job because of cutbacks at your company. A resilient person will look at this not as an obstacle to overcome, but as a new opportunity. Maybe this person has never had the time to look at other employment opportunities. Maybe this person will decide to go back to school to change careers. The difference between resilient people and others is that they perceive the challenges differently. Other people might be depressed and stressed over losing their job, but resilient people, though they might be stressed at first, have the ability to bounce back and use the challenge as a way to see and do things differently.

iQ PRACTICE Go online for more practice with using referents to understand contrast. *Practice > Unit 5 > Activity 6*

READING 2

OBJECTIVE ▶

The Climb of My Life

You are going to read an excerpt from a book called *The Climb of My Life: Scaling Mountains with a Borrowed Heart* by Kelly Perkins. It's about a woman who climbs a mountain ten months after having a heart transplant. A transplant is a type of surgery in which an organ, for example, a heart, liver, or kidney, is replaced. Use the reading to gather information and ideas for your Unit Assignment.

PREVIEW THE READING

A. PREVIEW Read the title and first two paragraphs. Why do you think Kelly Perkins felt that she needed to climb a mountain? Check (✓) your answer.

☐ She wanted to improve her health.

☐ She wanted to improve how she felt about herself.

☐ She likes the excitement of mountain climbing.

B. QUICK WRITE Think about a time when you had a challenge in life, perhaps a physical challenge like an illness. What did you do to help you overcome this challenge? Write for 5–10 minutes in response. Be sure to use this section for your Unit Assignment.

C. VOCABULARY Check (✓) the words you know. Use a dictionary to define any new or unknown words. Then discuss how the words will relate to the unit with a partner.

bravely *(adv.)*	distinctive *(adj.)* OPAL	role *(n.)* 𝔎 OPAL
conquer *(v.)*	earn *(v.)* 𝔎	significant *(adj.)* 𝔎 OPAL
determined *(adj.)* 𝔎	goal *(n.)* 𝔎 OPAL	ultimate *(adj.)* OPAL

𝔎 Oxford 3000™ words   OPAL Oxford Phrasal Academic Lexicon

iQ PRACTICE Go online to listen and practice your pronunciation.
Practice ⟩ Unit 5 ⟩ Activity 7

WORK WITH THE READING

🔊 **A. INVESTIGATE** Read the excerpt and gather information about why people take risks.

THE CLIMB OF MY LIFE

1   At the age of 30, Kelly Perkins developed a disease of the heart, and after three years of treatment, she received a heart transplant. Ten months later, she climbed to the top of Half Dome Mountain in Yosemite National Park in the United States and became the first heart transplant patient to do so.

2   Like life, mountains can be seen as a series of difficulties that you need to overcome. To me, a mountain is the **ultimate** challenge, with body, spirit, and mind all having to work together. Being sick is a challenge, too. Both challenges involve **bravely** facing the unknown, and to **conquer** either requires well-defined **goals** and discipline. Of the two, of course, I'd rather the mountain be my physical challenge than physical challenges be my "mountain."

3   Mountains began to consume my thoughts. Secretly, I wanted to do something **significant** to help change the image that friends and family had developed of me. I had been cast in the **role** of patient. In spite of being very good in that role, I hated being a patient and desperately wanted to change my image. I wanted bruises to be **earned** from sports-related activities, not from needle pricks and aspirin-thinned blood. At this stage, my self-image was as important to my well-being as anything else. If, I figured, I could rebuild my strength and regain at least some of my former athleticism, an improved image would naturally follow.

4   I set a goal—to hike the 4,100-foot ascent of Half Dome in Yosemite. I was drawn to this destination by its beauty, a beauty not because it was perfect, but because it was imperfect. Half Dome's shape is unforgettably **distinctive** because it's broken. If it were whole, it would lose its uniqueness. The spirit-building message wasn't lost on me. Just because I wasn't perfect didn't mean I couldn't stand as tall and mighty as anyone else.

5   In August of 1996, just ten months after my heart replacement, my husband Craig and I began to hike the trail leading to Half Dome. The trail began with a mild incline, which we eagerly took at a brisk pace. I was winded at first, but as soon as my heart caught up with me, I felt energized. I tried to go as fast as the other hikers, but found it difficult to keep up. The canyon had many steep slopes and deep stone stairs, allowing in very little sunlight, which kept temperatures cool and the rocks slippery.

6   Though the climb's final half-mile isn't technically difficult, the granite dome, angled at 45 degrees, can be extremely intimidating, especially for those afraid of heights. A stairway is used to climb the last 500 feet to the summit. There was a handrail made out of steel cables, connected to stairs made of thin wooden planks. Thrown along the stairs were weathered work gloves, available to help protect the climbers' hands from the "death grip" commonly used during descent. Craig, observing the daunting task ahead, gently asked, "Are you sure you want to continue?"

Determined to reap[1] the reward for all my effort, I replied, "Absolutely, we have to go on." Step for step, Craig stayed directly behind me, providing a welcome sense of security. When I finally reached the top, I was overcome with joy. Ten months after my transplant, I had reached the top of Half Dome! My new heart had not failed me.

7   Craig and I made our way over to the edge. Pausing to peer into the valley below, we stood in silence, amazed at how far we had come. As if the moment itself was not enough, Craig surprised me with a gold charm[2] in the shape of Half Dome. He said, "This is the first mountain to add to the bracelet I gave you." As I held the handcrafted ornament in my hand, I was amazed at its likeness. It was smooth on the back, resembling the perfectly bell-shaped dome, the front being chiseled, replicating its famous broken granite face. Craig took a moment to express how proud he was of me, saying, "When you were really sick and I had to help you up the stairs at night, I always looked at the famous Ansel Adams photo of Half Dome hung on the stairway wall and wondered if we'd ever make another climb." We had done it; we were here at the top of the mountain—a long way from those nights of not knowing what the future would bring.

---

[1] **reap:** to receive a benefit due to one's efforts
[2] **charm:** a small piece of jewelry often worn on bracelets

..., you learned
that synonyms are
words that have similar
meanings. Can you
think of any synonyms
for the vocabulary
words in Activity B?

B. VOCABULARY Complete each sentence with the vocabulary from
Reading 2.

bravely *(adv.)* 4   distinctive *(adj.)* 6   role *(n.)* 5 Position
overcome conquer *(v.)* 2   earn *(v.)* 7 get   significant *(adj.)* 9
determined *(adj.)* 3   goal *(n.)* 1   ultimate *(adj.)* 8 top very good

1. My _____ for this year is to train until I am ready to run the city
   marathon.

2. My husband took a class that helped him _____ his fear of
   flying. Now he can ride in airplanes without feeling so nervous.

3. We were very tired, but we didn't give up. We were _____
   to get to the top of the mountain.

4. The firefighters _____ entered the burning school to rescue
   the children.

5. When our parents were away, my oldest brother took on the
   _____ of the family guardian.

6. I always recognize Dina on the phone because she has a very
   _____ voice. She doesn't sound like any of my other friends.

7. When we were children, we had to do work around the house in order to
   _____ rewards like toys or candy.

8. Rock climbing is the _____ activity for people who want a
   fun, exciting challenge.

9. Volunteering in South America was one of the most _____
   experiences of my life. It inspired me to pursue a career in public service.

iQ PRACTICE Go online for more practice with the vocabulary.
Practice > Unit 5 > Activity 8

C. IDENTIFY Read the sentences. Then number them in the order that the
events happened.

_2_ 1. Perkins decided to climb Half Dome Mountain in Yosemite.

_4_ 2. Ten months after her heart replacement, Perkins began to climb
Half Dome.

_3_ 3. Perkins decided that she wanted to climb a mountain to change
her image.

_1_ 4. Kelly Perkins became very sick and received a heart transplant.

_6_ 5. Craig was proud of his wife's accomplishment.

_5_ 6. Perkins reached the top of Half Dome with a new heart.

D. INTERPRET Read the summary statements. Then write the number of the paragraph that each statement summarizes.

2 ___8___ 1. I'd prefer to be challenged by mountain climbing and not illness.

___4___ 2. I hoped to stand tall, but imperfect, like the mountain I chose to climb.

___6___ 3. The last part of the mountain is so steep that there are stairs to help people climb to the top, and I was going to be one of those people.

___3___ 4. I missed extreme physical activity and needed to prove to my family and friends, and more importantly, to myself, that I could still do it.

E. RESTATE Complete each statement with information from Reading 2. Then write the paragraph number where the answer is found.

1. Kelly Perkins chose a mountain to climb that is __4100__ feet high.
Paragraph: __4__

2. One reason she chose this mountain is because, like her, it is
__imperfect__. Paragraph: __4__

3. Perkins began her climb of Half Dome with her husband in August of __996__.
Paragraph: __5__

4. The last half-mile of the climb is hard if you're afraid of heights because it's angled at _____ degrees. Paragraph: ____   45   6

5. There is a rough stairway to help climbers for the last __500__ feet.
Paragraph: __6__

6. Perkins's husband Craig said it was the first mountain to add to a(n)
__braislet__ that he had given her. Paragraph: __7__

× **F. CATEGORIZE** Read the statements. Write *T* (true) or *F* (false) and the paragraph number where the answer is found. Then correct each false statement to make it true according to the article.

6 __F__ 1. Kelly Perkins didn't want her husband to climb directly behind her.
Paragraph: ____

7 __F__ 2. Craig was confident before this climb that they would be climbing mountains again. Paragraph: ____

5 __T__ 3. Perkins had trouble when she began the climb up Half Dome Mountain.
Paragraph: ____

3 __T__ 4. Perkins used to be very athletic before she got sick. Paragraph: ____

6 __F__ 5. The gloves on the stairs of Half Dome are to help people going up the mountain. Paragraph: ____

G. DISCUSS Discuss the questions in a group. Look back at your Quick Write on page 115 as you think about what you learned.

1. In paragraph 2, Kelly Perkins talks about challenges—climbing mountains and being sick—and says, "Of the two, of course, I'd rather the mountain be my physical challenge than physical challenges be my 'mountain.'"
   What does this mean for Perkins?

2. Perkins climbed mountains before and after her heart transplant.
   Do you think the reasons for climbing mountains were different before and after her transplant? Why or why not?

WORK WITH THE VIDEO

A. PREVIEW Did you ever have a bad experience doing something that made you fearful of doing it again?

VIDEO VOCABULARY

deal with (v. phr.) to act in a suitable way in order to solve a problem, complete a task, etc.; to handle something

control of (n. phr.) power over something; the ability to organize, direct, or guide somebody or something

panic (v.) to have a sudden feeling of fear that makes you act without thinking carefully

keep up with (v. phr.) to continue to do something to be on the same level as others

look forward to (v. phr.) to wait with pleasure for something to happen (because you expect to enjoy it)

iQ RESOURCES Go online to watch the video about a young girl named Shona, who is learning to ride a horse again after getting hurt. *Resources > Video > Unit 5 > Unit Video*

B. CATEGORIZE Watch the video two or three times. Then take notes in the first part of the chart.

	How Shona felt when she first arrived at the riding school	How she overcame her fear of riding
Notes from the video		
My ideas		

C. EXTEND What do you think was the biggest factor in helping Shona to overcome her fear? Write your ideas in the chart above.

WRITE WHAT YOU THINK

SYNTHESIZE Think about Reading 1, Reading 2, and the unit video as you discuss these questions. Then choose one question and write a paragraph in response.

1. Do you think that people who had very bad childhoods could forget about their past? In other words, do you think they need to move past their previous difficulties and focus on the present?

2. Do you think people can change the way they perceive challenges or obstacles? Are there certain situations or times in people's lives that we perceive as traumatic? Is there another way to look at these experiences?

VOCABULARY SKILL Using the dictionary to find the correct meaning

Words often have more than one meaning. When dictionaries include more than one meaning, the different definitions are usually numbered. When you are using a dictionary to find the **correct meaning** for a word, it is important to read the entire sentence and consider the context.

Look at the example and the dictionary definitions that follow it. Definition 4 is correct.

Mountains began to **consume** my thoughts.

> **con·sume** ⚘ Ⓦ /kən'sum/ *verb* [T] *(formal)* **1** to use something such as fuel, energy, or time: *25 percent of the world's population consumes 80 percent of the planet's resources.* **2** to eat or drink something: *to consume calories* **3** (used about fire) to destroy something **4** (used about an emotion) to affect someone very strongly: *She was consumed by grief when her son was killed.*

All dictionary entries adapted from the *Oxford American Dictionary for learners of English* © Oxford University Press 2011.

A. Read these sentences from the readings. Look up the underlined words in your dictionary and write the correct definition based on the context. Then compare your answers with a partner.

1. Do you <u>fall apart</u> or <u>rise</u> above it?

   fall apart: _2 - to have so many problems that it is no longer possible to exist or function_

   rise above: _to not be affected or limited by problems_

2. From a young age, resilient children tended to <u>meet</u> the world on their own terms.

   meet: _0 - to experience s/t often s/t unpleasant_

3. I had been cast in the <u>role</u> of patient. *actor*

role: <u>the function or position that s/b has</u>

4. I wanted bruises to be <u>earned</u> from sports-related activities, not from needle pricks and aspirin-thinned blood.

earned: <u>to get sth that you deserve</u>

5. It was smooth on the back, resembling the perfectly bell-shaped dome, the front being chiseled, replicating its famous broken granite <u>face</u>.

face: <u>s. aside or surface</u>

B. Choose three words from Activity A. Write a sentence using each word.

1. _____

_____

2. _____

_____

3. _____

_____

iQ PRACTICE Go online for more practice with using the dictionary to find the correct meaning. *Practice > Unit 5 > Activity 9*

WRITING

At the end of this unit, you will write a narrative essay about an obstacle that you have faced. This essay will include specific information from the readings, the unit video, and your own ideas.

WRITING SKILL Writing a narrative essay

A **narrative essay** tells the story of a personal experience or event. The introductory paragraph of a narrative essay gives necessary background information and then explains why this is an important or memorable story for the writer. This main idea is included in the thesis statement.

A narrative essay also contains the other important parts of an essay, including two to three body paragraphs and a concluding paragraph. The body paragraphs describe the events and include details, such as facts, examples, or explanations, to support the thesis statement or main idea of the essay. The concluding paragraph restates the main idea and summarizes why this story is an important one for the writer.

A. WRITING MODEL Read the model narrative essay.

When I graduated from college, I took a two-week vacation to the West Coast before starting my job as a teacher in New York City. My friend Sophia and I planned to drive up the coast from Los Angeles to San Francisco. It was the third day of the trip and our first day of rain. As I was driving up Route 1, the rain became heavier. Suddenly, a truck approached on the opposite side of the road. The truck was dangerously close to our car as we went around a sharp curve. And that's the last thing I remember. That day would change my life forever.

When I woke up, I was in a hospital in California. My parents were there, looking very concerned. I was a bit disoriented, and my mother explained that there had been a terrible accident. Sophia was fine and had gone home to her family. And I was going to be fine, though not completely. My right leg had been so damaged in the accident that they had to amputate it. I had lost my leg. I was completely devastated.

Over the next few months, I focused mainly on regaining my health. There were certainly ups and downs, but when I got depressed, my mom helped me see that I was lucky to be alive. As I got stronger, I had to learn to deal with having only one leg. When my injury had healed enough, I had to learn to walk again—with only one leg. It was very painful in the beginning. I tried not to think about how the rest of my life was going to unfold. I just focused on getting stronger and on learning to walk on my new leg, an artificial one.

About six months after my accident, I was ready to begin my new life. I had gotten fairly good at walking on my prosthetic leg, and I found out about a group that helped people deal with injuries like mine, Achilles International. They worked out together in Central Park every week. Since I had been a runner on the track team in college, it seemed like a good fit for me. Every month they had short races in Central Park. I thought, "What have I got to lose?" I finished my race, but more importantly, I had accomplished something that a few months before I had thought would be impossible. Also, I met people who I could help, people who had injuries or physical challenges far worse than mine. It helped me see that my injury, though very serious, was not really going to change my life. I would still be able to continue with my dreams and my life goals. It was just "a bump in the road of life" that I had to come to terms with.

It's now a year later, and I'm finally teaching in the school I had planned to be in a year ago. I have gotten accustomed to wearing my new leg and have even gotten another one, specifically for running. I'm still involved with Achilles International and plan to run the marathon this fall. I acknowledge that my life has changed, but I am still the same person inside.

B. EVALUATE Reread the narrative essay in Activity A. Then answer the questions.

1. Where does the writer give background information? Put a check mark (✓) next to it.

2. Which sentence in the introductory paragraph includes the main idea (thesis statement) of the narrative? Write it below.

_____

_____

3. How many body paragraphs does the writer include? Mark the body paragraph(s) with brackets. ([ ])

4. What details does the writer include to help show the passage of time. Underline them.

5. Which sentence in the concluding paragraph explains why this story is important to the writer? Write it below.

_____

_____

C. WRITING MODEL Read the model narrative essay. Then answer the questions below.

The storm began quickly and wildly. I was sitting in my living room watching the ocean as the waves grew in size and strength. Many people told me I was foolish to stay in my house and not seek shelter away from the beach. But this was my home. I had always stayed put during previous hurricanes, and this was no exception. _____

_____

The ferocious winds died down almost as quickly as they had started. As I inspected my house, I realized the basement contained two feet of water. Fortunately, I had removed anything valuable before the storm. Then I noticed the flood of water running down the street. The street was no more, replaced by a river running through the neighborhood. As I was surveying the area, I heard shouts from down the street. I walked out to the garage and grabbed my kayak. This would provide my transportation for the next few hours.

I paddled down the street to where the shouts were coming from. One of my neighbors had also stayed in his house, but the water had poured into the second floor. He and his family, including two small children, were left with only the attic to stay in. I tied a rope to each of the children and placed them into the kayak. I paddled them to the end of the street where the water subsided and pavement was visible. We finally reached an undamaged home, and I lifted the children to safety. Then I returned to help their parents.

Though the flooding went on through the night, the damage had been done in minutes. Some people thought I should not have stayed in the house, but saving my neighbor and his family was proof enough for me that I had made the right decision.

1. Which sentence is the best thesis statement for the essay? Discuss your choice with a partner. Write the thesis statement in the introductory paragraph.

   a. Hurricanes are very exciting, so I wanted to stay and see as much as I could.

   b. I felt confident that nothing was going to happen to my house, so I made my decision to stay and watch it.

   c. I knew it could be dangerous, but I thought maybe I could help others who might be in need.

2. Underline any background information in the introductory paragraph.

3. Look at the concluding paragraph. Underline the words that restate the main idea and summarize why this story is important to the writer.

iQ PRACTICE Go online for more practice with writing a narrative essay.
Practice > Unit 5 > Activity 10

A written essay or passage begins with a specific **time frame**, such as past, present, or future. Sometimes writers use one time frame for the entire passage, but often they shift or change time frames. Writers shift time frames according to what they are describing.

Writers often use the **simple past** to begin a story, or set the scene.

> simple past
> A few months after the Half Dome climb, I **decided** to climb Mt. Whitney in California.

Writers use the **past perfect** to describe things that happened before the events in the story. Use *had* + **past participle** to form the past perfect.

Present]. have
Perfect]. has

> simple past
> Secretly, I **wanted** to do something significant to help change the image that
>
> past perfect
> friends and family **had developed** of me.

Writers use the **simple present** to describe things or give certain facts or information.

> simple present   simple present
> Half Dome's shape **is** unforgettably distinctive because **it's** broken.

iQ RESOURCES Go online to watch the Grammar Skill Video.
Resources > Video > Unit 5 > Grammar Skill Video

A. IDENTIFY Look back at the model narrative essay on page 123. Draw a box around the simple past verbs and past perfect verbs. Circle the simple present verbs. Then compare your answers with a partner.

B. EXTEND Read the short passages. Write *present* if the passage uses only a present time frame. Write *past* if the passage uses only a past time frame. Write *present/past* or *past/present* if the passage changes time frames.

past/present   1. Three years ago, I went hiking in the White Mountains in New Hampshire. New Hampshire is a beautiful place to hike with lots of lakes and mountains.

_____   2. The storm last week caused a lot of damage, and many people could not get to work or school. Now the roads are clear, and businesses and schools are open again.

3. Florence, Italy, is a wonderful place to spend a vacation. There are lots of interesting things to do and see.

4. Last year, Amy decided to try rock climbing. It was something she had always wanted to try.

5. Mountain climbing is exciting, but it can be dangerous. Last year, there were hundreds of accidents.

C. COMPOSE Complete each sentence using a different time frame.

1. I used to drive to work, but now _I ride my bike_____.

2. I used to drink soda every day. Now _____.

3. When I was younger, I didn't speak English very well. Now _____
_____.

4. Many things are different in my country now. For example, in the
past, _____.

5. I used to eat every meal in a restaurant. I'm trying to save money,
so now _____.

6. I used to watch TV all weekend, but now _____.

iQ PRACTICE Go online for more practice with shifts between past and present time frames. *Practice › Unit 5 › Activities 11–12*

UNIT ASSIGNMENT Write a narrative essay

OBJECTIVE ▶

In this assignment, you are going to write a narrative essay about an obstacle that you have faced. Think about how you were able to overcome the obstacle. As you prepare your essay, think about the Unit Question, "How do people overcome obstacles?" Use information from Reading 1, Reading 2, the unit video, and your work in this unit to support your essay. Refer to the Self-Assessment checklist on page 128.

iQ PRACTICE Go online to the Writing Tutor to read a model narrative essay. *Practice › Unit 5 › Activity 13*

PLAN AND WRITE

A. BRAINSTORM Think of and write some obstacles or challenges that you've faced. They can be small or big. Write as many as you can.

B. PLAN Follow these steps to plan your essay.

1. Look at the obstacles you wrote down in Activity A. Choose one of the obstacles to write about for your essay.

2. Write your thesis statement.

iQ RESOURCES Go online to download and complete the outline for your narrative essay. *Resources > Writing Tools > Unit 5 > Outline*

C. WRITE Use your planning notes to write your essay.

1. Write your narrative essay describing an obstacle that you have faced.

2. Look at the Self-Assessment checklist below to guide your writing.

iQ PRACTICE Go online to the Writing Tutor to write your assignment. *Practice > Unit 5 > Activity 14*

REVISE AND EDIT

iQ RESOURCES Go online to download the peer review worksheet. *Resources > Writing Tools > Unit 5 > Peer Review Worksheet*

A. PEER REVIEW Read your partner's essay. Then use the peer review worksheet. Discuss the review with your partner.

B. REWRITE Based on your partner's review, revise and rewrite your essay.

C. EDIT Complete the Self-Assessment checklist as you prepare to write the final draft of your essay. Be prepared to hand in your work or discuss it in class.

SELF-ASSESSMENT	Yes	No
Does the essay begin with an introductory paragraph that describes the obstacle and any important background information?	☐	☐
Does the essay include two body paragraphs that describe the events and provide details?	☐	☐
Does the essay contain a concluding paragraph that restates your obstacle and how you overcame it, and summarizes why the story is important to you?	☐	☐
Does the essay shift between present and past correctly?	☐	☐
Are words used with the correct meaning?	☐	☐
Does the essay include vocabulary from the unit?	☐	☐
Did you check the essay for punctuation, spelling, and grammar?	☐	☐

D. REFLECT Discuss these questions with a partner or group.

1. What is something new you learned in this unit?

2. Look back at the Unit Question—How do people overcome obstacles? Is your answer different now than when you started the unit? If yes, how? Why?

iQ PRACTICE Go to the online discussion board to discuss the questions. *Practice > Unit 5 > Activity 15*

TRACK YOUR SUCCESS

iQ PRACTICE Go online to check the words and phrases you have learned in this unit. *Practice > Unit 5 > Activity 16*

Check (✓) the skills you learned. If you need more work on a skill, refer to the page(s) in parentheses.

CRITICAL THINKING	☐ I can justify my opinion of a text. (p. 110)
READING	☐ I can use referents to understand contrast. (p. 113)
VOCABULARY	☐ I can use the dictionary to find correct meanings. (p. 121)
WRITING	☐ I can write a narrative essay. (p. 123)
GRAMMAR	☐ I can use time shifts correctly in narrative writing. (p. 126)
OBJECTIVE ▶	☐ I can gather information and ideas to write a narrative essay about an obstacle that I've faced.

Neurology

6

READING	using a graphic organizer
CRITICAL THINKING	classifying information
VOCABULARY	phrasal verbs
WRITING	stating reasons and giving examples
GRAMMAR	gerunds and infinitives

Are you a good decision maker?

A. Discuss these questions with your classmates.

1. What is an important decision you made recently in your life? Was it a good decision?

2. Is it easy for you to make big decisions about your life, or is it difficult? Why?

3. Look at the photo. What decision is the man making?

B. Listen to *The Q Classroom* online. Take notes about each person in the chart.

	What decision did he or she make?	Was it a good or bad decision? Why?
Marcus	s/t depends to situation buy car	
Sophy	I think so Learn english	
Yuna	not recently- Park car learned	

iQ PRACTICE   Go to the online discussion board to discuss the Unit Question with your classmates. *Practice > Unit 6 > Activity 1*

UNIT OBJECTIVE

Read the articles and gather information and ideas to write an analysis essay about whether you are a good decision maker.

READING 1

OBJECTIVE ▶

The Lazy Brain

You are going to read an article from a science magazine about the effects of lazy thinking. Use the article to gather information and ideas for your Unit Assignment.

PREVIEW THE READING

A. PREVIEW Read the title. Read the caption under the first photograph. What do you think the title means by "the lazy brain"?

B. QUICK WRITE What was an important decision you made recently? Did you make the right decision? Write for 5–10 minutes in response. Be sure to use this section for your Unit Assignment.

C. VOCABULARY Check (✓) the words you know. Then work with a partner to locate each word in the reading. Use clues to help define the words you don't know. Check your definitions in the dictionary.

according to *(prep.)* 🔑 OPAL	**function** *(v.)* 🔑 OPAL	**proof** *(n.)* 🔑
complex *(adj.)* 🔑 OPAL	**make sense** *(v. phr.)*	**rely on** *(v. phr.)*
efficient *(adj.)* 🔑 OPAL	**pace** *(n.)* 🔑	**subject** *(n.)* OPAL
experiment *(n.)* 🔑 OPAL		

🔑 Oxford 3000™ words   **OPAL** Oxford Phrasal Academic Lexicon

iQ PRACTICE   Go online to listen and practice your pronunciation.
Practice ▶ Unit 6 ▶ Activity 2

WORK WITH THE READING

🔊 **A. INVESTIGATE** Read the article and gather information about whether you are a good decision maker.

THE LAZY BRAIN

The lazy brain prefers elevators.

1   If you are a lazy person, don't worry—you might be able to blame your brain! At least, that's what the research suggests.

2   Being lazy doesn't just mean you take the elevator instead of the stairs. It can also mean the way you think and make decisions is "lazy." The problem is that this all happens without our even knowing about it. So, what can we do about it? How can we make our brains less lazy?

3   To understand why the brain wants to be lazy, we must understand how the brain works. The brain is very **complex**, and it actually thinks in two different ways. The first way is the lazy way, and it is a good kind of lazy. It is the thinking we use when we add 1+1. It's the same lazy thinking we use when we drive to school or work. We don't have to think about how to do it—we just do it! **According to** scientists, we have thousands of these lazy thoughts every day.

4   So, why does the brain like lazy decisions? When we do things fast and we don't have to think, we save energy. The brain and body are always trying to save energy. If we save energy, we have more of it, and more energy means we can **function** better in the world. Think about how hard it is to think when we are tired or hungry. We make more mistakes because our brain is too tired.

5   In fact, research has shown that the brain is trying to save energy all the time. In an **experiment** at Simon Fraser University in Canada, scientists wanted to test how good the brain was at saving energy (Selinger et al. 2015). They asked nine **subjects** to walk on a treadmill. The subjects naturally walked at a **pace** that saved the most energy. Then the scientists made it more difficult. They added weight at the knees. As a result, the subjects' original pace was not the most **efficient** anymore. Immediately, they began to walk differently to save as much energy as possible. The brain was saving energy in real time. It happened without them even thinking about it.

6   So, it is good that the brain is lazy because it saves energy. But unfortunately, that's not the whole story. When people **rely on** lazy thinking in situations that require hard thinking, they can run into trouble.

7   For one, lazy thinkers are more likely to believe things without any **proof**. This means that they may accept that something is true even when it isn't. For example, let's say you meet someone new. He tells you, "I'm an honest person," and you assume he is. But in reality, he lies to people, even his friends. Unfortunately, your lazy brain doesn't let you question his honesty. You believe he's a good person because that was the easiest thought.

...are also more likely to make bad decisions. One research ...hat businesspeople with lazy brains have ended up making ... decisions. They didn't think things through; instead, they ...cisions based on their emotions. Their companies lost ...ne of them lost everything. This is often because people with lazy brains are too confident. Their lazy thinking makes them think they know everything when they really don't.

9 So, how can people fight lazy thinking? Luckily, there is a way. Humans also have another kind of thinking—"hard thinking"—but it takes a lot more energy. Hard thinking is slower. It's the kind of thinking we use when we solve a difficult problem, like 17 x 24. It's the kind of thinking we use when we make more difficult decisions, like when we decide on the career we want or where to live.

10 When we use hard thinking, the body isn't so happy because we are demanding a lot more energy from it. That explains why students get so tired after studying for a test. It explains why long conversations make people want to grab a cup of coffee. They need the caffeine because they feel like they're out of energy. They're not using their lazy brain anymore.

11 The problem is that many people don't use hard thinking enough, and that is what causes problems. So, the advice from scientists is to fight it. In other words, don't just accept everything you hear as true. Question it, and see if it really **makes sense** or not. Don't be too confident about what you know—remember that your first thoughts might be wrong, because they're from your lazy brain. Also, don't forget to take the stairs next time!

References

Selinger, J. et. al. 2015 "Humans Can Continuously Optimize Energetic Cost during Walking," *Current Biology*. September 21, 2015. doi: 10.1016/j.cub.2015.08.016

ACADEMIC LANGUAGE

The corpus shows that *according to* is more common in academic writing than academic speaking.

OPAL
Oxford Phrasal Academic Lexicon

B. VOCABULARY Here are some words from Reading 1. Read the sentences. Then write each bold word next to the correct definition on page 135. You may need to change the form of some of the words.

1. The human brain is able to solve both simple and very **complex** problems.

2. **According to** scientists, the brain works harder when people are sleeping than when they are awake.

3. The brain **functions** similarly to the way a computer works in that it stores information, solves problems, and makes decisions about what to do.

4. In an **experiment** at the University of Southern California, researchers found that studying music at a young age makes children's brains grow faster.

5. The **subjects** in the experiment were children in Los Angeles who received music instruction at school for free.

6. Generally, it is a good idea to walk at a quick **pace** because it makes the heart work harder and burns more calories.

7. Students who work have to find the most **efficient** ways to use their time so that they can have enough time to study and do their homework.

8. People who **rely** too much **on** first impressions can make bad judgments about who someone really is. It takes time to really get to know how another person thinks.

9. Some people believe that dreams are the brain's way of solving problems, but it is very difficult to find **proof** for that because we can't study dreams easily.

10. If the brain likes being lazy, it **makes sense** that people want to get from one place to another in the shortest distance possible.

4 a. _____ (n.) a scientific test that is done in order to study what happens and to gain new knowledge

6 b. _____ (n.) the speed at which somebody walks, runs, or moves

3 c. _____ (v.) to perform a particular job or role

9 d. _____xo_____ (n.) information, documents, etc., that show that something is true

1 e. _____ (adj.) difficult to understand or deal with

5 f. _____ (n.) a person being used to study something, especially in an experiment

2 g. _____ (prep.) as stated or reported by someone or something

8 h. _____ (v. phr.) to trust or have confidence in somebody or something

10 i. _____ (v. phr.) to have a meaning that can be understood

7 j. _____ (adj.) doing something well and with no waste of time, money, or energy

iQ PRACTICE Go online for more practice with the vocabulary.
Practice > Unit 6 > Activity 3

C. IDENTIFY Circle the main idea of the article.

a. Lazy thinkers are more likely to make bad decisions about money and finances.

b. Some people have more lazy thoughts than others, but it is not their fault.

c. The lazy brain helps people save energy, but it can also cause bad decisions.

d. According to scientists, people are trying to save energy all the time.

D. CATEGORIZE Read the statements. Write *T* (true) or *F* (false). Then correct each false statement to make it true according to the article.

T ____ 1. People have hundreds of lazy thoughts a day.

F ____ 2. Lazy thinkers often believe things that are not true.

F ____ 3. When people have lazy brains, they don't feel confident about their decisions.

T ____ 4. The subjects in the experiment decided to change their pace.

T ____ 5. Choosing a career is an example of hard thinking.

F ____ 6. When people solve difficult math problems, they are using less energy.

T ____ 7. One way to fight lazy thinking is to think faster.

E. EXPLAIN Answer the questions. Write the paragraph number where the answer is found.

lazy   *3* 1. What kind of thinking do people use when they drive? Paragraph: ____

_____

to save energy *4* 2. Why does the brain make lazy decisions? Paragraph: ____

_____

10 3. How is hard thinking different from lazy thinking? Paragraph: ____

_____

_____

hard thinking *9* 4. What advice do scientists give about how to fight lazy thinking? Paragraph: ____

_____

_____

F. ANALYZE Read each situation. Check (✓) if you think the situation uses lazy thinking or hard thinking. Compare your answers with a partner.

	Lazy thinking	Hard thinking
1. driving to the store	☐ ✓	☐
2. reading a textbook	☐	☐ ✓
3. choosing a college	☐	☐ ✓
4. making coffee	☐ ✓	☐
5. buying milk at the store	☐ ✓	☐
6. multiplying 14 x 19	☐	☐ ✓
7. giving a friend advice	☐	☐ ✓
8. choosing a seat on the bus	☐ ✓	☐

G. DISCUSS Work with a partner. Make a list of decisions you made today. Which ones do you think were lazy? Which ones were not lazy?

iQ PRACTICE Go online for additional reading and comprehension.
Practice > Unit 6 > Activity 4

WRITE WHAT YOU THINK

A. DISCUSS Discuss the questions in a group. Think about the Unit Question, "Are you a good decision maker?"

1. Do you think you are a lazy thinker when you make decisions? Why or why not?

2. When did you make a decision using hard thinking? Was it a good decision?

3. When you meet someone new, can you tell if the person is honest or not? How?

B. COMPOSE Choose one of the questions from Activity A and write a paragraph in response. Look back at your Quick Write on page 132 as you think about what you learned.

when I make a decision, I think alot about that, because I want to be sure my decision is good. I research and ask about my~~id~~ of people who have experience about what I want todo. when I am at least 90% sure about that, I do my decision.

Graphic organizers represent ideas with images, such as diagrams, charts, tables, and timelines. You can use graphic organizers to help you see connections between ideas or remember the main points of a text or parts of a text. Drawing graphic organizers can help you review a text you have read in preparation for class or a test.

Scientific articles often show cause-effect or reason-result relationships. This reason-result organizer shows the relationship between a reason and its different results.

Results

Reason

| The brain wants to save energy. | People choose the elevator. |
| People walk at the most efficient pace. |
| People do things fast. |

TIP FOR SUCCESS

Looking for patterns of organization in a text will help you understand what the writer wants to say about the topic.

A. CATEGORIZE Write the ideas from Reading 1 into the graphic organizer to illustrate the main reasons and results.

People make bad decisions. *Result*

People feel too confident. *Result*

People have lazy thinking. *Reason*

People believe things without proof. *Result*

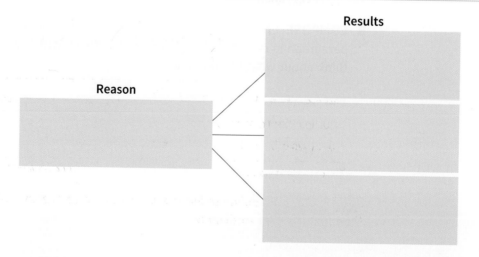

Results

Reason

B. EXTEND Work with a partner. Read the paragraph from Reading 1. Make a reason-result graphic organizer to illustrate the main reason and its results.

Reason

When we use hard thinking, the body isn't so happy because we are *Reason* demanding *Result* a lot more energy from it. That explains why students get so tired after *Reason* studying for a test. It explains why long conversations make people want to *Result* grab a cup of coffee. They need the caffeine because they feel like they're out of energy. They're not using their lazy brain anymore.

iQ PRACTICE Go online for more practice with using a graphic organizer.
Practice > Unit 6 > Activity 5

READING 2

Problem-Solvers: Which One Are You?

OBJECTIVE ▶

You are going to read a magazine article about different ways people solve problems. Use the article to gather information and ideas for your Unit Assignment.

PREVIEW THE READING

A. PREVIEW Read the title of the article and skim the first two paragraphs. What is the purpose of the article? Check (✓) your answer.

☑ to explain how people solve problems in different ways

☐ to describe the kinds of problems people have at work

☐ to suggest why some people are more creative than others

B. QUICK WRITE When you have an assignment to do at school or work, do you prefer to work alone, in a small group, or in a big group? Why? Write for 5–10 minutes in response. Be sure to use this section for your Unit Assignment.

C. VOCABULARY Check (✓) the words you know. Then work with a partner to locate each word in the reading.

arrogant *(adj.)*	have a gift *(v. phr.)*	revolutionary *(adj.)*
come up with *(v. phr.)*	impatient *(adj.)* ⚲	view *(v.)* ⚲ OPAL
deal with *(v. phr.)*	move on *(v. phr.)*	

⚲ Oxford 3000™ words   OPAL Oxford Phrasal Academic Lexicon

iQ PRACTICE Go online to listen and practice your pronunciation.
Practice > Unit 6 > Activity 6

WORK WITH THE READING

 A. INVESTIGATE Read the article and gather information about how different kinds of people make decisions.

PROBLEM SOLVERS:
WHICH ONE ARE YOU?

1   At school, at work, in life—you're always solving problems. How you solve a problem may be very different from the way others do. You might want to fix it quickly, but others want to take their time. You might have a lot of creative ideas, but you take a lot of time to make decisions.

2   The way people think about problems varies greatly. Everyone is unique, but psychologists believe there are about five different kinds of problem-solvers in the world. And knowing which one you are can have a big impact on your ability to work with other people successfully. So, which one sounds the most like you?

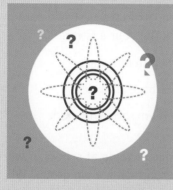

QUESTIONERS

3   Questioners are people who think hard about a problem. They ask many questions to themselves and to others. The more complex the problem is, the more questions they will ask about it. Sometimes they even answer people's questions with a question. They want to make sure they have thought about everything before making a decision. Questioners are good because their questions make other people think harder, too. But the problem is these problem-solvers can also be very slow to solve a problem.

IDEATORS

4   Ideators are the idea people. They're the most creative thinkers in the room. They can easily influence people because their ideas are so unique, and people are impressed by their minds. Because Ideators **have a gift**, their solutions can be truly **revolutionary**. The negative side is that they can sometimes annoy other people because they care less about finding a solution. They think of lots of solutions, and some of them may never work. So they're slower decision makers.

DIGGERS

5   Diggers are good to have on a team because they think about all the details. They want to "dig into" a problem and break it down so they can see all of the facts. When they have them all, then they can make their final decision. Consequently, they usually feel very confident about their choices. However, they can be slow at making decisions, and they may not offer their opinions to others until the very end. This can make other people wrongly assume that they aren't really working on the problem.

DOERS

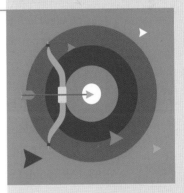

6   For Doers, getting to a solution quickly is very important. They don't spend as much time asking questions or digging into problems. They prefer to focus on the present because they don't want to waste time thinking about the past. They try to keep things moving along in the right direction. Sometimes, Doers don't even wait to find the complete solution. For them, it's OK to just solve part of the problem and **move on**. So, Doers are excellent at solving things quickly, but sometimes other people see them as too **impatient**.

REASONERS

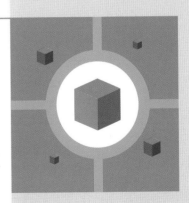

7   Reasoners are the people who like to keep things simple. When they **deal with** a complex problem, they prefer to focus on the most important elements. They don't want to worry about small details, which means they solve problems more quickly than other people. Also, for Reasoners, the "best" solution is the solution that they **came up with**. Unfortunately, they also have creat a hard time listening to other people's ideas. As a result, people sometimes see Reasoners as too confident or **arrogant**.

8   When you figure out what kind of problem-solver you are, you can understand how you think. Perhaps more importantly, you will also begin to see how other people **view** you. That is very important because teamwork is one of the most important skills people need to succeed in today's world. In college, students are constantly asked to work in groups and do team projects. At work, you'll be a part of many teams, and you'll need to come to solutions together. When you know the strengths and your weaknesses of your thinking, you will be able to work with others to solve problems even more successfully.

B. VOCABULARY Here are some words from Reading 2. Read the definitions. Then complete each sentence with the correct word.

Sav 1.
arrogant *(adj.)* behaving in a proud or unpleasant way, showing little thought for other people

Creat a plan = 8 **come up with** *(v. phr.)* to find or produce an answer, a sum of money, etc.

5 **deal with** *(v. phr.)* to solve a problem, solve a task, etc.

gifted = talent — 6 **have a gift** *(v. phr.)* to be very good at doing something

4 **impatient** *(adj.)* annoyed or irritated by someone or something, especially because you have to wait for a long time

3 **move on** *(v. phr.)* to start doing or discussing something new

2 **revolutionary** *(adj.)* involving a great or complete change

7 **view** *(v.)* to have a personal opinion about or particular attitude toward something

arrogant 1. John is a very _____ person. He always thinks he has the best ideas, and he never thinks he is wrong.

2. The president of the college had a(n) _____ idea to provide free day care for students with young children.

3. Although I was not very happy with my test results, I decided to _____ and begin thinking about how to do better on the next one.

4. Sometimes my coworker can be very _____. He has trouble waiting for things, and he prefers to get projects done early, even if they aren't perfect.

5. My mother and father _____ problems very differently. My father usually makes decisions on his own, but my mother prefers to ask friends for their advice first.

6. My daughters both _____ for the arts. One is a successful painter, and the other plays the violin in an orchestra.

7. Many people _____ the boss as someone you should listen to and not disagree with, but in my opinion, it's good to speak up when you have a different point of view.

8. Even though Sami is only 13, he has already _____ a plan to study medicine and become a doctor when he gets older.

iQ PRACTICE Go online for more practice with the vocabulary.
Practice > Unit 6 > Activity 7

C. IDENTIFY What is the main idea of the article? Circle the answer.

a. People are always solving problems in their lives, but some people take more time to solve problems than other people.

✓ b. Understanding the personalities of different kinds of problem-solvers can help people be more successful when working with others.

c. Teamwork has become one of the most important skills in the workplace and at school because people always work in groups.

d. Reasoners and Doers prefer to solve problems slowly, but Diggers, Ideators, and Questioners take more time making decisions.

D. CATEGORIZE Read each set of positive and negative characteristics. Then write the type of problem-solver they describe.

Type of problem-solver	Positive characteristic	Negative characteristic
1.	They solve problems very quickly.	They can be impatient.
2.	They help other people think more.	They solve problems slower than others.
3.	They are able to see all the details of a problem.	They are slow to give their opinion about a solution.
4.	They are able to solve problems faster than others.	They can be seen as arrogant.
5.	They come up with ideas that no one else thinks about.	They can annoy people who want a real solution.

Handwritten notes in margin: Doers, Reasoners, Questioner, ideatds, diggers, reasoners, reasoners ideators, diggers, Questioners; × teamwork; ×

E. EVALUATE Look at the positive and negative characteristics of the five categories of people in Activity D. How are the types similar and different? With a partner, use the phrases below to state the similarities and differences.

Handwritten: They think better

(Questioners) and (Ideators) are similar because . . .

(Questioners) and (Ideators) are different because . . .

F. IDENTIFY Read these sentences from Reading 2. Then answer the questions. Find the sentences in the reading to help you.

1. (Paragraph 1) You might want to fix **it** quickly, but others want to take their time.

   What does *it* refer to? _____ Problems _____

2. (Paragraph 3) **They** want to make sure they have thought about everything before making a decision.

   Who does *they* refer to? ___ | Questioner _____

3. (Paragraph 4) **They** can easily influence people because their ideas are so unique.

   Who does *they* refer to? ___ 2 ideator _____

4. (Paragraph 4) They think of lots of solutions, and some of **them** may never work.

   What does *them* refer to? _____

5. (Paragraph 5) When they have **them** all, then they can make their final decision.

   What does *them* refer to? _____

6. (Paragraph 6) For **them**, it's OK to just solve part of the problem and move on.

   Who does *them* refer to? _____

CRITICAL THINKING STRATEGY

Classifying information

When you **classify** information, you arrange ideas into different types or categories according to how they are similar to each other. For example, in Reading 2, the author classified people into five different problem-solving types to show what is special about each one. When you classify, you are better able to see similarities and differences among the categories.

iQ PRACTICE Go online to watch the Critical Thinking Video and check your comprehension. *Practice > Unit 6 > Activity 8*

G. CATEGORIZE Read about the different problem-solvers. Classify them according to the type of problem-solver they are. Go back to Reading 2 to help you.

_____I_____ 1. Everybody loves Rodolfo! He has the most interesting ideas, and he's always thinking of new ways to do something. The only problem is sometimes he doesn't stay focused on the real problem.

_____di_____ 2. Maryam is really good to have on our team because she helps us break down a problem into the smallest parts. Then each of us can work on a different detail at a time. Unfortunately, sometimes she can take a long time to figure out what those details are.

_____do_____ 3. Norbert is the guy you want on your team if you want something done on time. In fact, he's so fast that he usually finishes his projects early! Norbert is good for me because sometimes I am just way too slow at completing a project.

_____U_____ 4. Rushi is such a patient person! He will go over and over and over something until he finds the answer he's looking for. Sometimes I say to him, "Well, what do you think?" His response? "I know what I think, but what do _you_ think?"

_____R_____ 5. Bridget is an interesting person. She's very smart, and she can deal with all kinds of problems, from simple to complex. However, she often doesn't really hear what other people are trying to say, and that can upset them.

H. COMPOSE What kind of problem-solver do you think like the most? Write a paragraph of 5–8 sentences in response.

WORK WITH THE VIDEO

A. PREVIEW Is it possible to know when something good or bad will happen before it happens? Share your opinion with a partner.

VIDEO VOCABULARY

crew (n.) all the people working on a ship, plane, firetruck, etc.

backdraft (n.) an explosion caused by more oxygen being supplied to a fire, for example, by a door being opened

intuition (n.) the feeling or understanding that makes you believe or know something without any reason or proof

subconsciously (adv.) connected with feelings that influence your behavior even though you are not aware of them

iQ RESOURCES Go online to watch the video about intuition.
Resources > Video > Unit 6 > Unit Video

B. IDENTIFY Watch the video two or three times. Then choose the correct answers.

1. Andy Kirk had a *normal / strange* feeling.

2. Andy told the firefighters to *enter / leave* the building.

3. The color of the smoke was *gray / orange*.

4. Air was rushing *out of / into* the building

5. There was *a lot of / no* sound from the fire.

6. Andy's *conscious / subconscious* mind saved people's lives.

C. EXTEND The video suggests that people can make good decisions to help others very quickly in an emergency situation. What is an example of a quick decision you've made that helped someone?

WRITE WHAT YOU THINK

SYNTHESIZE Think about Reading 1, Reading 2, and the unit video as you discuss these questions. Then choose one question and write a paragraph in response.

1. Think about a friend or family member who usually makes good decisions. Why do you think he or she is a good decision maker?

2. What are factors that can make people make bad decisions? Are they factors people can control or not control?

3. Do you think people generally think only one way, or is it possible for someone to think in many different ways?

VOCABULARY SKILL Phrasal verbs

A **phrasal verb** is a combination of a verb and a particle. Particles are usually prepositions, such as *up, on, in, down,* and *over*. When they are combined with a verb, however, they can change the meaning of the verb.

Compare these pairs of sentences:

The company recently decided to **move** its main headquarters from Los Angeles to Toronto, Canada.

When Jack finishes a project, he likes to **move on** right away to the next one so he doesn't waste time.

According to the rules of the game, I had to **deal** everyone seven cards and place the rest of the cards on the table.

When I have lots of things to do, I prefer to **deal with** the hardest thing first and then go on to the easier ones.

The phrasal verb *move on* has a different meaning from the verb *move*.

move → to change the place where you live or have your work

move on → to start doing or discussing something new

The phrasal verb *deal with* has a different meaning from the verb *deal*.

deal → to give cards to each player in a game of cards

deal with → to take action in order to solve a problem or complete a task

prepositional phrase : preposition + (modifiers) noun

under the desk

in my very larg bag → desk

A. INTERPRET Match each phrasal verb with its definition below. Look back at the readings to help you.

C ___ 1. run into (Reading 1, Paragraph 6)

b ___ 2. end up (Reading 1, Paragraph 8)

a ___ 3. think through (Reading 1, Paragraph 8)

e ___ 4. break down (Reading 2, Paragraph 5)

d ___ 5. move along (Reading 2, Paragraph 6)

f ___ 6. figure out (Reading 2, Paragraph 8)

a. to think about something until you understand it   3

b. to find yourself in a place or situation that you did not intend or expect to be in   2

c. to experience problems   1

d. to keep something going   5

e. to separate things into parts in order to analyze it or make it easier to do   4

f. to consider a problem or a possible course of action fully   6

B. APPLY Complete each sentence with the correct phrasal verb from Activity A.

2 1. I want to complete the project by the end of the day, but I think I will _____ having to bring it home to finish it.

6 2. It was difficult for her to _____ the answer to the question   6 because she didn't understand a lot of the vocabulary in the text.

4 3. My algebra teacher has the ability to _____ a complex math   4 problem into smaller pieces so students can understand it better.

1 4. Some people _____ trouble when they make the wrong   1 judgment about someone new they meet.

5 5. Doers want to make sure that things _____ quickly so that they   5 can find a solution and not waste time.

3 6. The teenager didn't _____ all of the consequences of his   3 actions. As a result, he made a big mistake and got into trouble with his parents.

iQ PRACTICE Go online for more practice with phrasal verbs.
Practice > Unit 6 > Activity 9

WRITING

At the end of this unit, you will write an analysis essay using reas~ about whether you're a good decision maker. This essay will incl~ information from the readings, the unit video, and your own ide~

WRITING SKILL Stating reasons and giving examples

An **analysis essay** is a piece of writing that carefully examines a topic by breaking it down into smaller parts. The writer looks at the smaller parts in separate body paragraphs and explains them so the reader will understand the main topic. To help explain the topic and pieces, the writer states reasons and gives examples.

Writers state **reasons** to explain why something happens or is true. Reasons can explain why people act or do things in a certain way or why things happen. Writers support their reasons with **examples**. Examples can be specific situations, observations, or personal experiences that writers give to make their reasons clear.

> **Thesis statement** (situation): In my opinion, I think a lot like a Doer.
>
> **Topic sentence** (Reason 1): One reason I'm a Doer is because I prefer to focus on the present.
>
> **Example:** I try not to worry about past mistakes that I've made in my life.
>
> **Example:** I don't think a lot about the future because it's impossible to predict what will happen.
>
> **Topic sentence** (Reason 2): Another reason I'm a Doer is because I like to make decisions quickly.
>
> **Example:** I don't like wasting hours shopping for the perfect piece of clothing.
>
> **Example:** I always know exactly what I want when I go out to eat at restaurants.

There are certain phrases that signal examples, such as *for example* and *for instance*.

Stating reasons with *because*

Because is often used to show reasons why something happens or is true. When *because* is at the beginning of a sentence, a comma is put before the second subject-verb combination.

> reason   second subject-verb combination
> Because I spent more time with my grandmother, I think the most like her.

When *because* is in the middle of a sentence, no comma is used.

>   reason
> Our boss made a bad decision because he didn't consider all of the facts.

A. WRITING MODEL Read the model analysis essay. Underline the thesis statement in paragraph 1 and the topic sentences in paragraphs 2–4.

My Mother, Myself

1   I have a very loving mother. When I was young, we spent a lot of time together because she quit her job after I was born. She taught me how to walk, how to read, and how to be a good and honest person. Now I am in college, and I appreciate all of the time I was able to spend with her. I know now that my mother has had a very big influence on the way I think. We think a lot alike in the way we question things, deal with mistakes, and make decisions.

2   One reason my mother and I are similar is because we are both Questioners. We are very curious about life, and we always want to know more. We are more likely to answer each other's questions with another question instead of an actual answer. For example, the other day, my mother asked me, "Do you think I should cut my hair short?" I responded, "Well, do you want shorter hair, or do you like your hair long?" I preferred her hair long, but I didn't tell her that. I wanted her to discover the answer herself. The questions we ask each other help us solve problems because we make each other really think about our decisions. With my mother, no question is ever a bad question.

3   Another reason I think like my mother is because we both think too much about the past. For instance, when I make a mistake, it is hard for me to forget about it. I usually think about what I did for a long time. I think about what I could have done better. For example, if I made someone upset, I think about what I could have said differently to not make him or her angry. I have a hard time getting over mistakes. The problem with this is that I sometimes can't focus on the present. For instance, when I am with my friends and we are having fun, I might still be thinking about a mistake I made earlier that day, but then I don't enjoy the experience as much. I definitely get this trait from my mother. She always worries about past mistakes even though she knows they can't be changed.

4   Finally, both my mother and I are slow when it comes to making important decisions. Because we're both natural Diggers, we both like to think things through for a long time before we decide to take action. For example, I recently moved out from my parents' house, and I had to decide what kind of apartment to get. I didn't want to just take the first one I saw. In fact, I looked at over 15 apartments before I decided on the one. I had to get all the facts: the price, the size, the neighborhood. Then I had to compare everything to choose the best apartment. My mother was with me the whole time, and she was digging through the facts just as much as I was. This meant that it took a little long to finally decide, but in the end, we were both confident about my decision.

5   All in all, there are a lot of reasons why I think like my mother. Because we're both Questioners and Diggers, we help each other think more deeply about life. However, nobody is perfect, and we both struggle sometimes with thinking too much in the past and not focusing enough on the present. Still, I am very proud to carry on the same thinking that my mother has given me. We are definitely not lazy thinkers, and that's probably why we've both been able to lead happy, successful lives.

B. CATEGORIZE Complete the graphic organizer with information from the essay in Activity A.

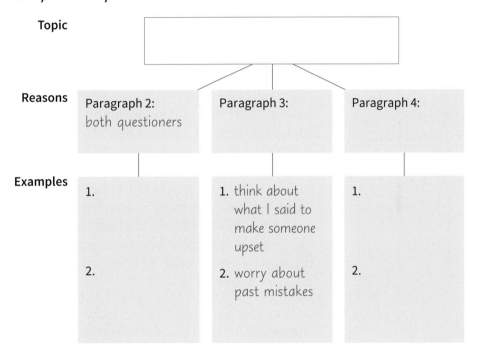

Topic

Reasons

Paragraph 2:
both questioners

Paragraph 3:

Paragraph 4:

Examples

1.

2.

1. think about what I said to make someone upset

2. worry about past mistakes

1.

2.

C. WRITING MODEL Read the model analysis essay. On page 152, match the examples with the reason in each body paragraph.

Being a Digger

1   I have always loved numbers. I am an accountant, and I currently work for a large bank in Toronto, Canada. I work with a team of about 20 people, and all of us bring something different to the table. We all have our own personalities, and we don't all solve problems the same way. When I think about how I solve problems, I definitely consider myself a Digger.

2   One reason I'm a Digger is because I'm very detail-oriented. For example, when I am with my coworkers, I am listening to what everyone is saying and writing down all the important points. Later, I go back and

review my notes to make sure I have everything. If I am missing any information, I will go back to the person to get it because I want all the facts. Sometimes this annoys people because they think that I wasn't really listening to them.

3   Another reason I'm a Digger is because I don't give my opinions right away. When I am in a meeting at work, I do not talk as much as other people. I will only speak up when I'm totally confident about what I have to say. I don't want to waste people's time just telling them the first thing that comes to my mind. I also like to think about what people are saying and reflect on that, so I usually don't always give my opinions at meetings. This doesn't mean I never share them, however. Often, I will talk to people later to give them my reflections and explain how I feel.

4   Finally, I'm a Digger because I am slow at making decisions. At work, people always want things fast. Every morning, we receive an email from our boss telling us all the things that need to be completed that day and by the end of the week. When I see the list, I can get a little nervous. It's not that I don't start working on things right away. I work hard and I take my job very seriously, but I just need more time to think because I need things to be perfect.

5   All in all, I think I'm definitely a Digger. I like to break problems down so that I have all the information I need to share my opinions or make decisions. Sometimes being a Digger can annoy my coworkers who like to solve problems immediately, but I also recognize that it has its strengths, too. People always know they can come to me for information they're missing because I probably have it down somewhere. And if I don't have it, I know how to dig for it.

____ Paragraph 2   ____ Paragraph 3   ____ Paragraph 4

a. For example, I can't even send a coworker an email until I am sure that it says exactly what I'm thinking.

b. For example, last week my coworker got a little upset with me for asking for the same information again, but I just wanted to be sure I understood it.

c. For example, I often email my coworkers the day after a meeting to share my opinion about how to solve a problem.

D. IDENTIFY Read the sentences. Underline the reasons. Add commas if needed.

1. Because Diggers get all of the facts they feel more confident about their decisions.

2. Because the businesspeople made bad decisions their companies lost a lot of money.

3. The scientists performed an experiment because they wanted to prove theory.

4. Hard thinking takes more energy because the brain is working a lot m[...]

5. Because the subjects were using lazy thinking they changed their pace without knowing.

6. Reasoners are good to have on a team because they can help solve problems quickly.

iQ PRACTICE Go online for more practice with stating reasons and giving examples. *Practice > Unit 6 > Activity 10*

GRAMMAR Gerunds and infinitives

A **gerund** is the base form of a **verb + -ing**. Gerunds can function as nouns in a sentence. A gerund can be one word (*running, eating, living*) or part of a phrase (*running outdoors, eating healthily, living in a big city*).

Gerunds as subjects

A **gerund** or **gerund phrase** can be the subject of a sentence. A gerund subject always takes a singular verb.

> **Thinking** <u>is</u> easier and faster when we use our lazy brain.
> **Being lazy** <u>doesn't</u> just <u>mean</u> you take the elevator instead of the stairs.

Gerunds after verbs

Gerunds follow certain verbs. Here are some of the verbs that gerunds follow.

> avoid   discuss   enjoy   go   quit
> consider   dislike   finish   practice   suggest

An **infinitive** is *to* + **the base form** of a verb. Infinitives can function as objects in sentences.

> Doers want **to solve** a problem as quickly as possible.

Infinitives follow certain verbs. Here are some of the verbs that infinitives follow.

> agree   decide   hope   plan   wait
> appear   forget   learn   seem   want

iQ RESOURCES Go online to watch the Grammar Skill Video.
Resources > Video > Unit 6 > Grammar Skill Video

A. COMPOSE Complete each sentence with a gerund phrase. Use the words in parentheses.

1. _Understanding human behavior_ (understand/human behavior) is not always easy.

2. _____ (be/a good listener) is a very important skill to have.

3. _____ (use/lazy thinking) can cause people to make bad decisions.

4. _____ (get/enough sleep) is crucial to your brain's health.

5. _____ (solve/complex problems) takes more time and effort.

B. APPLY Complete each sentence with a verb + a gerund. Use the words in parentheses.

1. I want to be healthier, but I really _dislike exercising_ (dislike/exercise).

2. If you have heart problems, you should _____ (quit/eat) salty foods.

3. Ahmed _____ (consider/move) to Riyadh, but he decided to stay in Jeddah.

4. We should _____ (avoid/buy) a big car because gasoline is too expensive.

5. Today we will _____ (discuss/write) paragraphs.

6. After Margo _____ (finish/eat) dinner, she read the newspaper.

C. APPLY Complete each sentence with a gerund or an infinitive. Use the verb in parentheses.

1. I hope _____to go_____ (go) to Australia someday.

2. Yuri wants _____ (visit) his friend in Seoul next fall.

3. You should practice _____ (speak) Spanish every day.

4. My neighbor agreed _____ (help) me fix my car.

5. Do you enjoy _____ (play) soccer?

6. Jamal goes _____ (swim) every morning with his son.

iQ PRACTICE   Go online for more practice with gerunds and infinitives.
Practice > Unit 6 > Activities 11–12

UNIT ASSIGNMENT Write an analysis essay with reasons and examples

OBJECTIVE ▶

In this assignment, you are going to write an analysis essay using reasons and examples. As you prepare to write, think about the Unit Question, "Are you a good decision maker?" Use information from Reading 1, Reading 2, the unit video, and your work in this unit to support your paragraph. Refer to the Self-Assessment checklist on page 156.

iQ RESOURCES Go online to the Writing Tutor to read a model analysis essay. *Practice ⟩ Unit 6 ⟩ Activity 13*

PLAN AND WRITE

A. BRAINSTORM Follow these steps to help you organize your ideas.

1. Think about the ways you make decisions about things that have happened in your life. Brainstorm reasons why you make good or bad decisions.

2. Brainstorm examples for your reasons in Step 1. Think about example situations and personal observations you can use to make your reasons clearer.

_____

_____

3. Think about the readings and video in this unit. Is there any information that can help support your ideas?

B. PLAN Write a thesis statement for your analysis essay.

_____

_____

iQ RESOURCES Go online to download and complete the outline for your analysis essay. *Resources ⟩ Writing Tools ⟩ Unit 6 ⟩ Outline*

C. WRITE Use your planning notes to write your essay.

1. Write your analysis essay that explains how you make decisions. Be sure to use reasons and examples to support your thesis statement.

2. Look at the Self-Assessment checklist on page 156 to guide your writing.

iQ PRACTICE Go online to the Writing Tutor to write your assignment. *Practice ⟩ Unit 6 ⟩ Activity 14*

REVISE AND EDIT

iQ RESOURCES Go online to download the peer review worksheet.
Resources > Writing Tools > Unit 6 > Peer Review Worksheet

A. PEER REVIEW Read your partner's essay. Then use the peer review worksheet. Discuss the review with your partner.

B. REWRITE Based on your partner's review, revise and rewrite your essay.

C. EDIT Complete the Self-Assessment checklist as you prepare to write the final draft of your essay. Be prepared to hand in your work or discuss it in class.

SELF-ASSESSMENT	Yes	No
Does the introductory paragraph include a thesis statement?	☐	☐
Does the essay include a body paragraph for each reason?	☐	☐
Does the essay contain examples to support the reasons?	☐	☐
Is *because* used correctly to state reasons? Are commas used if necessary?	☐	☐
Are gerunds with *-ing* forms used correctly?	☐	☐
Are all gerund subjects followed by a singular verb?	☐	☐
Does the essay contain phrasal verbs from the unit? Are they used correctly?	☐	☐
Does the essay include vocabulary from the unit?	☐	☐
Did you check the essay for grammar, punctuation, and spelling?	☐	☐

D. REFLECT Discuss these questions with a partner or group.

1. What is something new you learned in this unit?

2. Look back at the Unit Question—Are you a good decision maker? Is your answer different now than it was when you started the unit? If yes, how is it different? Why?

iQ PRACTICE Go to the online discussion board to discuss the questions.
Practice > Unit 6 > Activity 15

TRACK YOUR SUCCESS

iQ PRACTICE Go online to check the words and phrases you have learned in the unit. *Practice > Unit 6 > Activity 16*

Check (✓) the skills and strategies you learned. If you need more work on a skill, refer to the page(s) in parentheses.

READING	☐ I can use a graphic organizer. (p. 138)
CRITICAL THINKING	☐ I can classify information. (p. 144)
VOCABULARY	☐ I can use phrasal verbs. (p. 147)
WRITING	☐ I can state reasons and give examples. (p. 149)
GRAMMAR	☐ I can use gerunds and infinitives. (p. 153)

OBJECTIVE ▶ ☐ I can gather information and ideas to write an analysis essay about whether I'm a good decision maker.

Economics

READING	using a timeline
CRITICAL THINKING	adding details to support statements
VOCABULARY	collocations with verbs
WRITING	writing a cause/effect essay
GRAMMAR	complex sentences

Can a business earn money while making a difference?

A. Discuss these questions with your classmates.

1. Have you ever thought about starting your own business? If yes, what kind of business would you like to have?

2. When you buy something, do you think about the company that you are purchasing from? For example, are you curious about where and how the products are made?

3. Look at the photo. What product do you think is being sold here?

B. Listen to *The Q Classroom* online. Then answer these questions.

1. Felix thinks that companies can earn money while making a difference. But he thinks it's important to have a good business plan. Do you agree? What kind of product or service can you imagine writing a business plan for?

2. Yuna says that she supports companies that have a social component. She wants the companies to succeed. How do you feel about this? Do you ever buy products because you know the company is doing something for the community?

iQ PRACTICE Go to the online discussion board to discuss the Unit Question with your classmates. *Practice > Unit 7 > Activity 1*

UNIT OBJECTIVE

Read the articles and gather information and ideas to write a cause/effect essay about how a business can make money while making a difference.

READING 1

FEED Projects: How a Bag Can Feed Children in Many Ways

OBJECTIVE ▶

You are going to read a magazine article about social entrepreneurship, or a business that earns money and also makes a difference in the world. Use the article to gather information and ideas for your Unit Assignment.

PREVIEW THE READING

A. PREVIEW Read the title. How do you think this company will feed children?

B. QUICK WRITE Think about successful businesses. How do they earn money? What could they do with some of their profits to help others? Write for 5–10 minutes in response. Remember to use this section for your Unit Assignment.

C. VOCABULARY Check (✓) the words you know. Then work with a partner to locate each word in the reading. Use clues to help define the words you don't know. Check your definitions in the dictionary.

desire *(n.)* 🔑 OPAL	massive *(adj.)* 🔑	reusable *(adj.)*
distribute *(v.)* 🔑 OPAL	opportunity *(n.)* 🔑 OPAL	signify *(v.)*
estimate *(v.)* 🔑 OPAL	overall *(adj.)* 🔑 OPAL	
firsthand *(adv.)*	prospect *(n.)* 🔑	

🔑 Oxford 3000™ words   **OPAL** Oxford Phrasal Academic Lexicon

iQ PRACTICE Go online to listen and practice your pronunciation.
Practice > Unit 7 > Activity 2

WORK WITH THE READING

🔊 **A. INVESTIGATE** Read the article and gather information about how a business earns money while making a difference.

Lauren Bush Lauren giving a schoolchild a meal

⬤ FEED Projects:

How a Bag Can Feed Children in Many Ways

1. In 2004, when Lauren Bush Lauren was in college, she was a volunteer for the UN World Food Programme (WFP). This gave her the **opportunity** to travel to various countries around the world. She traveled to countries like Chad in Africa and Guatemala in Central America. In her travels, she saw **firsthand** the hunger that exists in many parts of the world. More significantly, she saw how hunger affects children. She also saw how important a school lunch was to these children. As she told a reporter for *Forbes*, " . . . a free school meal not only nourishes a child, but it provides a reason for them to go to school every day and stay in school longer. This means opportunity for equal education and better job **prospects**. While traveling with the WFP, I've witnessed how the school lunch is truly a community event. The mothers who come to help prepare the meal are able to eat, as well as their other children who are not yet school-aged."

2. Bush Lauren was affected by what she had seen, and she wanted to do something to help. After graduating from college in 2005, she kept thinking about how to help those children. Always interested in fashion and design, she came up with a way to combine her interest in design and her **desire** to help feed hungry children. She would create a bag to raise money for feeding the hungry.

3. At that time, **reusable** bags were becoming popular. Bush Lauren realized that if she designed a bag that could be reused, people might be interested in buying it. They might be more interested if they knew that their purchase would help feed hungry children. She partnered with Ellen Gustafson, who worked for the WFP at the time, and in 2007, FEED Projects was born.

4. That first bag was made of all natural products and looked similar to the bags that the UN had used to **distribute** food. It also had the number 1 on it. That number **signified** one year of school lunches a child would receive from that purchase. FEED worked with the WFP to distribute the meals to children in schools. Consumers knew that their purchase of the bag meant that a child would receive a meal every day for a year.

5. This was the first of many bags in the social business FEED. The bags became very popular and the company grew. Bush Lauren continued to design more bags with numbers on them signifying the number of school lunches that would be provided for each bag purchased. A percentage of the retail price of the bags sold is spent on feeding the hungry. This money then goes to organizations like the WFP to distribute the meals.

6. The impact of feeding the hungry is very powerful. Today over 795 million people are affected by hunger around the world. It has been

shown that when children are given a nutritious meal, they perform better in school. Their education improves, giving them a better chance of improving their lives. Providing nutrition improves not only the child's education, but also their **overall** health. Malnutrition, or not getting the right nutrition to meet your body's needs, is a major cause of disease and illness globally. By providing a child with one meal a day, malnutrition is greatly reduced.

7   It should be noted that hunger is not just a problem in developing countries. It is also a problem in the United States, where it is **estimated** that 42 million Americans lack food. In 2013, FEED started a program with the organization Feeding America to provide nutritious school lunches to children in poor communities in the United States.

8   FEED has continued to expand and grow. Today the company produces many different bags in different materials. Their products also include jewelry and scarves. Many of these products are made by local artisans, thus providing employment for people in those countries. Currently FEED provides meals in 63 countries, in Africa and Central America, as well as in the United States. In 2017, the first FEED cafe and shop opened in Brooklyn, New York. As of 2018, FEED had provided more than 100 million lunches to children.

9   The problem of world hunger can't be solved overnight, but FEED has taken small but noticeable steps. As Bush Lauren said, "Global hunger . . . can seem like a **massive** problem, but I started FEED because I hoped that by providing people with a . . . way to make a difference, they would be able to better understand the problem and participate in the solution . . . I've learned that people want to get involved . . . They just aren't always sure where to begin." And through FEED, she has given them a way to start.

ACADEMIC LANGUAGE

The corpus shows that *it has been shown that* is often used in academic writing.

_____ OPAL

Oxford Phrasal Academic Lexicon

B. VOCABULARY Here are some words from Reading 1. Read the sentences. Then write each bold word next to the correct definition on page 163.

1. The **opportunity** to learn about business was very exciting to her.

2. His **overall** experience working at the marketing company was good, but he wanted to explore other work options.

3. I bought a bottle that is **reusable**. It's important to me to not create more waste.

4. When you have an internship, you can experience **firsthand** what it's like to work at a company.

5. The wildfire became **massive**, extending for more than 30,000 acres of the forest.

6. She achieved excellent grades in college, so the **prospect** of her getting a job was good.

7. The United Nations and other organizations **estimate** that over
   today live in poverty.

8. Many young people today have the **desire** to work in compan
   to the community in some way.

9. Sali will have a performance review next week. This will **signify** whe...
   doing well at her job or not.

10. Non-government organizations **distribute** food and medicine to people in need
    around the world.

a. _____10_____ (v.) to transport or supply something to various people
   or places

b. _____7_____ (v.) to calculate the size, cost, etc., of something

c. _____9_____ (v.) to be a sign of something; to mean

d. _____8_____ (n.) the feeling of wanting something very much; a
   strong wish

e. _____1_____ (n.) a chance to do something you would like to do

f. _____6_____ (n.) a chance or hope that something will happen

g. _____4_____ (adj.) heard, seen, or learned directly, not from
   other people

h. _____5_____ (adj.) very big

i. _____2_____ (adj.) including everything

j. _____3_____ (adj.) that can be used again

iQ PRACTICE Go online for more practice with the vocabulary.
Practice > Unit 7 > Activity 3

C. IDENTIFY Read the main ideas. Write the paragraph number where they
are found.

_2_ 1. Lauren Bush Lauren found an idea for combining her love of fashion and
       her desire to help the hungry.

_4_ 2. The bag with the number 1 on it was the first bag that FEED made.

_1_ 3. After traveling with the UN WFP, Bush Lauren saw how important a
       school lunch was to hungry children.

_7_ 4. FEED also works in the United States, where there are many hungry
       people.

_9_ 5. Bush Lauren founded her business because she wanted to give people a
       way to help solve the problem of hunger.

_6_ 6. Providing a school lunch has a great impact on a child, such as improving
       their health.

D. CATEGORIZE Read the statements. Write *T* (true) or *F* (false). Then correct each false statement to make it true according to the article.

F __ 1. Lauren Bush Lauren traveled to countries around the world with the UN World Food Programme after she graduated from college.

T __ 2. A free meal helps children stay in school.

F __ 3. The first bag designed for FEED had the number 1 on it signifying one lunch for a child in need. *one year*

T __ 4. A percentage of the profits from the sale of bags goes to feeding hungry children.

T __ 5. FEED distributes meals to schoolchildren in 63 countries of the world.

F __ 6. The company has expanded and now includes items like scarves *jewelry* and shoes.

E. INTERPRET Look more closely at the reading and answer the following questions. Write the sentence(s) that provide the answers.

1. What are other ways that a free school meal can "feed" children, according to the article? *education, health (6)*

   _education, health (6)_____

   _____

2. In what ways can a school lunch be a "community event"?

   mothers came to help for making food

   _____

3. Many founders of organizations have what is called an *aha moment* when they finally come up with an idea that they have been thinking about for a long time. What was Bush Lauren's aha moment?

   when she came up in a way to compine her interest
   in design and her disire to help feed hungry children.

4. Give an example of the global impact of feeding children.

   _America feed African children_____

   _____

F. EXTEND Look back at your Quick Write on page 160. Can you think of other products a company might sell to earn money and do good? Add any new ideas or information you learned from the reading.

iQ PRACTICE Go online for additional reading and comprehension.
Practice > Unit 7 > Activity 4

contamination

WRITE WHAT YOU THINK

A. DISCUSS Discuss the questions in a group. Think about the Unit Question, "Can a business earn money while making a difference?"

1. Lauren Bush Lauren saw a need that she felt passionate about. Is there any global problem that you feel passionate about?

2. Many social enterprises are able to fund their social cause by charging more for their products. Do you think this is a good way to raise money? Would you pay more to buy a product because it has a social impact?

B. CREATE Choose one of the questions from Activity A and write a paragraph in response. Look back at your Quick Write on page 160 as you think about what you learned.

READING SKILL Using a timeline

Creating a **timeline** can be useful for understanding and remembering the events in a text. A timeline should show all of the important events that happened during a period of time. Look at the timeline for Reading 1.

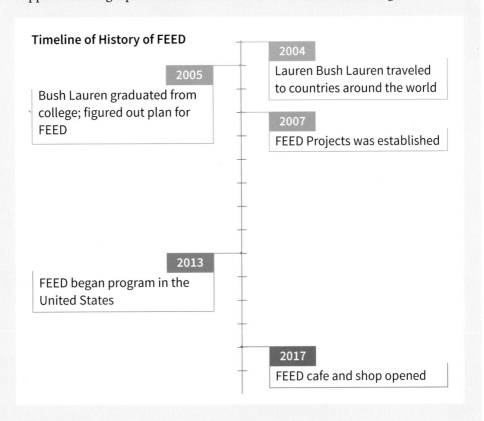

Timeline of History of FEED

- **2004** Lauren Bush Lauren traveled to countries around the world
- **2005** Bush Lauren graduated from college; figured out plan for FEED
- **2007** FEED Projects was established
- **2013** FEED began program in the United States
- **2017** FEED cafe and shop opened

iQ RESOURCES Go online to watch the Reading Skill Video.
Resources > Video > Unit 7 > Reading Skill Video

A. INVESTIGATE Read the article. Then complete the timeline. Use the sentences from the box.

Did you know that spending a few dollars on a bottle of salad dressing can help children with serious illnesses enjoy a week at summer camp? It's true, thanks to Newman's Own.

In December 1980, Paul Newman, a well-known American film actor, and his friend A.E. Hotchner made gallons of salad dressing to give to family and friends as gifts. Their friends loved it and wanted more, so Newman and Hotchner made more. But this time, they decided to bottle it and sell it. And the rest, as they say, is history. Newman's Own was born.

By the end of 1982, the first year of production, the profits were close to $400,000. It was a hit! Since neither Newman nor Hotchner needed money, Newman said, "Let's give it all away to those who need it." Over the years Newman's Own added different kinds of products. Newman died in 2008, but his business still carries on with 100 percent of the profits donated to charities. By the end of 2018, there were over 300 products sold, and more than $500 million had been donated to charities.

The company donates to various charities, but the one perhaps closest to Newman's heart is the Hole in the Wall Gang camp, founded in 1988. This special camp is designed specifically for seriously ill children. For one week, these children can forget about their illnesses and enjoy themselves. Their medical needs are taken care of, and since they are all sick, the children don't have to feel "different." Because of Newman's Own Foundation, all of this is provided free for the campers. It's all paid for by people buying salad dressing—a small price for such a great reward.

The Hole in the Wall Gang camp was founded.
Paul Newman died.
Newman and Hotchner made salad dressing for gifts.
More than 300 products were sold.
Profits were close to $400,000.

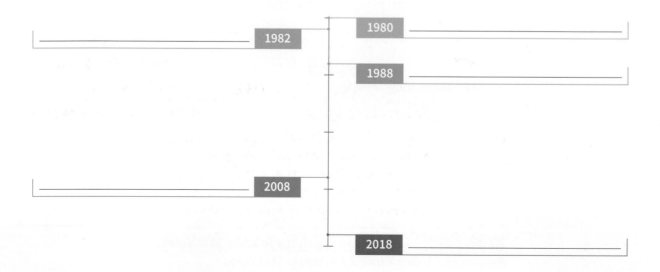

iQ PRACTICE Go online for more practice with using a timeline.
Practice > Unit 7 > Activity 5

READING 2

A New Business Model: Do Well While Doing Good

OBJECTIVE ▶

You are going to read an article from a business magazine about how businesses can earn money and do good. Use the article to gather information and ideas for your Unit Assignment.

PREVIEW THE READING

A. PREVIEW Look at the title and headings. What do you think the article is going to tell us about businesses that want to help others? Check (✓) your answer.

☐ Companies are having a hard time making money while helping others.

☐ Consumers are interested in the kinds of products social enterprises offer.

✓☐ Entrepreneurs have figured out ways to help others by doing more than just donating goods.

B. QUICK WRITE Why do businesses want to help others? Are consumers different today than in previous times? Write for 5–10 minutes in response. Be sure to use this section for your Unit Assignment.

C. VOCABULARY Check (✓) the words you know. Use a dictionary to define any new or unknown words. Then discuss how the words will relate to the unit with a partner.

Pay attention (verb)
things (N)

address *(v.)* 🍂 OPAL	**focus** *(n.)* 🍂 OPAL	**model** *(n.)* 🍂 OPAL
aspect *(n.)* 🍂 OPAL	**give back** *(v. phr.)*	**movement** *(n.)* 🍂 OPAL
concerned *(adj.)* 🍂 OPAL	**inspired** *(adj.)*	**seek** *(v.)* 🍂 OPAL

🍂 Oxford 3000™ words   OPAL Oxford Phrasal Academic Lexicon

I am bored
It is boring
worried or feeling

iQ PRACTICE Go online to listen and practice your pronunciation.
Practice > Unit 7 > Activity 6

WORK WITH THE READING

 A. INVESTIGATE Read the article and gather information about how businesses can earn money and do good.

Home   ABOUT   LATEST POSTS   ARCHIVES   🔍   Sign in   SUBSCRIBE

A NEW BUSINESS MODEL: DO WELL WHILE DOING GOOD

1   In the business world today, there is a growing **movement** to include a social component in a company's business plan. More and more young entrepreneurs feel the need to **give back** to the community in some way, and they've included this **aspect** in the companies that they are establishing.

Why the change?

2   Some say that it's the young people who feel differently about their futures. They don't want their work to be just about making money. Many young business people feel the desire to help others while fulfilling their own dreams of having a successful company.

3   And they've seen other successful stories to guide them, for example, lifestyle brand TOMS started in 2006. This is a company that was established on the principle of "One for One®." This means that when you purchase one of their products—for example, shoes—the company will donate a new pair to a child in need. So the company is based on a principle in which it has a product that earns them money but also allows them to give back to people. As of 2018, it employed around 500 employees and gave away 86 million pairs of shoes, provided 600,000 sight restorations, and helped secure 600,000 weeks of safe water to many communities around the world.

4   Many consumers also like the idea of giving back to the community. In a recent survey, 66 percent of people said they would pay more for an item if the company was doing social good with their purchases. It makes consumers feel good because they are indirectly helping someone in need by their purchase.

Children in TOMS shoes

From footwear to eyeglasses

5   It's not just a simple product that is the **focus** of these social ventures. Another company, Warby Parker, sells eyeglasses. They also help people in developing countries to see better. Using the one-for-one **model**, Warby Parker donates a pair of eyeglasses for every pair of Warby Parker eyeglasses purchased. (As of 2018, 2 million pairs of glasses had been donated. The company is valued at $1.75 billion.) In addition to eyeglasses, the company works with partners both in the U.S. and in developing countries that provide vision tests and glasses for children and adults. One of their

partners, VisionSpring, has provided vision tests and eyeglasses to millions of people around the world. The impact of all of this is easy to see. When a person's vision is improved, he or she will be able to learn better in school or be able to get a job and work better. This improves life for individuals and the overall economy of a particular area.

Nokero lights

How it works

6   With most social enterprises, there is a legitimate business of selling either goods or services. These companies are clearly for-profit businesses. From the profits of the goods sold, the company is able to donate goods or services to others around the world. Very often, the price of the goods bought is much higher than the goods provided, but as has been noted, people are willing to pay more for a product or service if they know that this is benefiting society in some way. The important difference between for-profit and social businesses is that the social give-back element is built into the business model of social entrepreneurship. You could say it's part of its DNA.

Different models

7   Some companies do not necessarily donate goods, but focus on global issues, such as the environment. One company, Nokero, has invented and produces very efficient solar lights. The name of the company means *no kerosene*. The company's mission is to eliminate the use of kerosene around the world. There are an estimated 1.2 billion people in the world that have no electricity. They rely on kerosene for both cooking and lighting. Kerosene is a very dangerous material, easily causing fires. It is also a major pollutant of the air. Nokero tries to **address** this problem. It provides people with an alternative to kerosene. They sell their lights to NGOs[1] at greatly reduced prices. The NGOs then distribute the lights to areas of need. The company tries to solve a global problem, but also is profitable. In 2015, it had earned $2 million in revenue.

8   Another environmental social venture is United by Blue. The company was started by a scuba diver who was **concerned** about the growing amount of plastic and other garbage in the oceans. He started a clothing company, and for each purchase, the company will clean a pound of garbage from "the world's oceans and waterways." To date, the company has cleaned over a million pounds of garbage from the water.

What they have in common

9   All of the founders of these social enterprises have a few qualities in common. First, they saw a problem and thought of a creative way to address it. Second, they are enthusiastic, even passionate about their cause. In addition, they are determined to make their company work. To this end, they **seek** experienced people to help them meet their goals. And finally, social entrepreneurs feel **inspired** by their work, especially when they see the results of their efforts firsthand. This is probably what keeps them, and their companies, going.

[1]**NGO:** non-government organization

B. VOCABULARY Complete the paragraph with the vocabulary from Reading 2. You may need to change the form of some of the words.

address *(v.)*	focus *(n.)*	model *(n.)*
aspect *(n.)*	give back *(v. phr.)*	movement *(n.)*
concerned *(adj.)*	inspired *(adj.)*	seek *(v.)*

I recently read about a company that is a social enterprise. I went to the store to buy some cleaning products. I was **concerned** about all
1
of the chemicals listed on the back of some of these products. Then I saw a product that claimed to be free of such ingredients. When I got home, I looked up the company on the Internet. It seems that the company was established by two college friends who were also **seeking** natural cleaning
2
products. Their story is quite interesting. They started making the products in their bathtub. After selling some of the products on the Internet, they started this company that has as its **focus** the elimination of
3
chemicals from the environment. Their business **model** has a
4
social **aspect** *(a part)* built into it. They want to eliminate toxic products
5
from the environment. Through their company, they are making a small dent *impact*
in doing so. They were one of the earlier businesses involved in a growing
(to do) *(Num) dictionary*
movement to do social good. They **address** the issue
6   7
of climate change by creating "green" products. They have even constructed their latest office in the greenest possible way. I feel **inspired**
8
by their story and hope I can use my skills to start a company that can also
give it back to society.
9

group of people

iQ PRACTICE Go online for more practice with the vocabulary.
Practice > Unit 7 > Activity 7

(to supporting) to provide help or financial assistance

C. APPLY Complete the statements from Reading 2. Circle the correct answer.

1. In paragraph 5, line 1, the word *ventures* most likely means ___.

   ✓ a. new businesses

   b. trips

   c. products

2. In the last line of paragraph 5, the word *this* refers to ___.

   a. the amount of money the company earns

   b. getting cheap eyeglasses

   ✓ c. providing vision tests and eyeglasses to millions of people

3. in paragraph 3, line 8, *give back* most likely means ___.

   a. return

   ✓ b. provide help

   c. get money

4. In paragraph 7, line 6, *this problem* refers to ___.

   ✓ a. how kerosene is dangerous and pollutes the air

   b. not enough food

   c. not enough water

5. Look back at the title of the article. *Do Well* most likely means ___.

   ✓ a. start a business

   b. be successful

   c. get a job

6. *Doing Good* most likely means ___.

   a. helping others

   b. earning money

   ✓ c. being successful

D. IDENTIFY Complete the main ideas from Reading 2. Use the phrases from the box.

3 has donated millions of shoes to people in need
6 feel inspired to continue
4 like the idea of giving back
5 provide light and reduce pollution
2 make a difference in the world
1 is built into their business model

1. One of the reasons that the business model has changed is that many consumers

   _____.

2. Young business people feel differently about making money and want to

   _____.

3. TOMS is an example of a for-profit business that

   _____.

4. The difference between for-profit companies and social businesses is that in social enterprises, the social give-back element

   _____.

5. Nokero produces efficient solar lights which they sell at reduced prices to NGOs and, in this way, can

   _____.

6. One quality of social entrepreneurs is that when they see the results of their work, they

   _____.

E. CATEGORIZE Complete the chart with the information from the box: the problem or situation that the business founders saw, what they sell, and the effect or result.

pollution in oceans

people can't see/
   vision problems

pollution and fires

~~kids have no shoes~~

~~shoes~~

clothes

eyeglasses

solar lights

~~poor people have shoes~~

cleaner oceans and waterways

people have light after dark;
   less danger/pollution

people get glasses/
   have better vision

	Problem/Situation	What they sell	Effect/Result
1. TOMS	kids have no shoes	shoes	poor people have shoes
2. Nokero	Pollution and fires	Solar Lights	People have light after dark; less danger/pollution
3. United by Blue		⟩	
4. Warby Parker	People can't See/vision problems	eyeglasses	People get glasses/ have better vision

F. SYNTHESIZE Discuss the questions in a group.

1. The article discusses a few reasons why the business model has changed. What are these reasons? Do you agree with the author about the reasons for the change? Which reason do you think is the most important?

2. Which person in Reading 2 do you feel the most inspired by? Why?

3. What are some of the qualities that the founders of social businesses have? Do you have any of these qualities? Are there any other qualities that you think are important to be a successful businessperson?

 CRITICAL THINKING STRATEGY

Adding details to support statements

When you add **details** to your writing, it helps the reader understand the points or examples you are explaining. One way to add details is to add a follow-up sentence. Look at the chart.

Example	Detail
Hunger is also a problem in the U.S.	It is estimated that 42 million people lack food.
The first bag had a number on it.	That number signified one year of school lunches for one child.

iQ PRACTICE Go online to watch the Critical Thinking Video and check your comprehension. *Practice ⟩ Unit 7 ⟩ Activity 8*

G. IDENTIFY Read these sentences from Reading 2. In the reading, underline the details that support each sentence. Then choose one of the companies described and go online to find a supporting article about the company.

1. So the company is based on a principle in which it has a product that earns them money, but also allows them to give back to people.

2. Many consumers also like the idea of giving back to the community.

3. Using the one-for-one model, Warby Parker donates a pair of eyeglasses for every pair of Warby Parker eyeglasses purchased.

4. The company tries to solve a global problem, but also is profitable.

5. He started a clothing company, and for each purchase, the company will clean a pound of garbage from "the world's oceans and waterways."

resorces

WORK WITH THE VIDEO

A. PREVIEW Do you know what ecotourism is?

VIDEO VOCABULARY

wildlife (n.) animals and plants that live in natural conditions

conservation (n.) the protection of the natural world

alternative (n.) one of two things that you can choose between

vested interest (n. phr.) a strong reason, especially one related to money, for wanting something to happen

iQ RESOURCES Go online to watch the video about ecotourism in Namibia, Africa. *Resources > Video > Unit 7 > Unit Video*

B. CATEGORIZE Watch the video two or three times. Then take notes in the first part of the chart.

	Problems in Namibia	Effects of ecotourism on Namibia
Notes from the video	Tourism depends on seeing wildlife economy depends on Tourism	They helped for economy in Namibia People understood that having animals in their area is better saving the animals life than hunt them
My ideas	People don't have knodlege to how make money and certainly their government are not responsible about economy	

C. EXTEND What are some global effects of ecotourism? Write your ideas in the chart above.

WRITE WHAT YOU THINK

SYNTHESIZE Think about Reading 1, Reading 2, and the unit video as you discuss these questions. Then choose one question and write a paragraph in response.

1. After reading about social entrepreneurship, do you think that businesses can be successful and also do good in the world? Why? Why not?

2. Why are social entrepreneurs inspired by seeing their work do good for others? How does this differ from other entrepreneurs?

3. In addition to its main focus, TOMS also provides medical care to people. It has also established factories in poor areas, thus providing jobs. Why do you think social entrepreneurs do additional work like this?

VOCABULARY SKILL Collocations with verbs

Collocations are words that are frequently used together. Learning collocations can improve your vocabulary and can help your writing sound more natural. Look at the examples of collocations with the verbs *provide* and *address*.

A free school meal <u>provides a way for children</u> to get healthy.

Solar lamps <u>provide an alternative to kerosene</u>.

Lauren Bush Lauren's company <u>addresses the issue of child hunger</u>.

Social entrepreneurs find creative ways to <u>address social problems</u>.

A. IDENTIFY Locate other examples of collocations with the verbs *provide* and *address* in Readings 1 and 2.

B. APPLY Complete the sentences with a form of the verb *address* or *provide*.

1. Many young students hope to _____ climate change.

2. Working from home _____ an alternative for new parents.

3. The organization arranges transportation, and this _____ a way for workers to get to their jobs.

4. Growing sales of the clothing help the company _____ the problem of pollution of oceans.

5. Having a job that paid her a decent wage _____ her with a reason to get up each morning.

iQ PRACTICE Go online for more practice with collocations with verbs.
Practice > Unit 7 > Activity 9

WRITING

OBJECTIVE ▶   At the end of this unit, you will write a cause/effect essay about how a business can do good. This essay will include specific information from the readings, the unit video, and your own ideas.

WRITING SKILL   Writing a cause/effect essay

A **cause/effect essay** analyzes the causes (reasons) and effects (results) of a situation or event. A cause/effect essay includes an introductory paragraph, body paragraphs, and a concluding paragraph.

In a cause/effect essay, the introductory paragraph describes the situation or cause, gives background information, and includes a thesis statement (main idea).

The thesis statement in a cause/effect essay describes the effects of the situation.

The body paragraphs of an essay provide support for the thesis statement. In a cause/effect essay, each body paragraph includes a topic sentence that states a supporting point and describes an effect. Other sentences in a body paragraph provide examples, details, or facts.

In a cause/effect essay, the concluding paragraph restates the main idea and often offers some additional thoughts or predictions for the future.

A. WRITING MODEL Read the model cause/effect essay. Underline the thesis statement.

1   When I was in college, I took a class in social economics. We discussed many social problems and brainstormed ways to address them. It was a good way for us to see that we have the power to make changes in the world. I started thinking about social problems in the area where I live. The issue that I saw was the lack of public transportation. I knew of many people who were unable to get to their jobs easily because of the poor public transportation system. Often, they could not afford to have a car. This lack of transportation seemed like a huge problem that I wanted to try to address.

2   I kept thinking about how to find a way to solve this problem. I know many people have cars and don't use them that much. There are also a lot of retired people in my town. I thought maybe I could combine these two groups of people: the ones who had difficulty getting to work and the "seniors" who were retired and had cars sitting in their driveways.

3   I decided to go on social media to find out if there were retired people who might like to help out. The response was amazing! There were many retired men and women who really didn't do that much and were

happy to help drive people to their jobs. I started making lists and maps of where the jobs were, how many people needed transportation, and how many seniors were willing to help. It all started to come together. I matched the drivers with the workers, and both were happy!

4   Now, six months later, I have a carpooling service. I have a steady and growing group of seniors who drive people to work. I have two shifts, one in the morning and one in the evening. (Some seniors prefer not to drive when it's dark.) As of now, the carpool has been successful in getting 25 workers to and from work every day.

5   There has been an additional benefit that I could not have foreseen. The seniors and the workers have become friends. Perhaps their lives would never have crossed if it weren't for this program, but now they help each other out in many ways. For example, one worker is very handy, and he helped a senior fix a broken cabinet in his home. This was an unexpected outcome, and it inspires me to continue with my carpooling project!

B. EXTEND Complete the graphic organizer with information from the essay in Activity A.

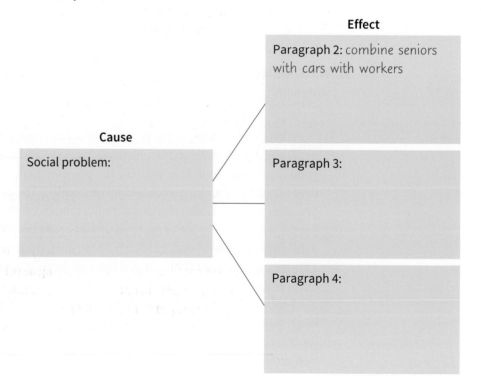

Effect

Paragraph 2: combine seniors with cars with workers

Cause

Social problem:

Paragraph 3:

Paragraph 4:

1   In 2006, Blake Mycoskie was traveling in South America and noticed that many children there had no shoes. Mycoskie soon found out that shoes are very important to people around the world. Owning a pair of new shoes may not seem like a really big thing to most of us. However, in many poor parts of the world, it *is* a big thing. Owning shoes can have a great impact on people's health, education, and well-being.

2   In many parts of the world, it is fairly common to see people, especially children, walking without shoes. However, there are many dangers to children when they do not wear shoes. In different parts of the world, many diseases, such as hookworm, can be contracted through the feet. Additionally, you can cut your feet on rough terrain or broken glass, which, in some cases, can lead to infection and risk of death. Finally, some climates are quite cold, and lack of footwear can lead to illness. So by simply owning a pair of shoes, a child's health is maintained.

3   A second, and perhaps more important, effect of owning a pair of shoes involves education. In many countries around the world, schools are not free. Parents must pay school fees and provide their children with uniforms, including shoes, in order for them to attend school. In some countries, children are not permitted to go to school if they don't have shoes. An additional benefit to owning a pair of shoes is that a child will be able to go to school.

4   Finally, when children receive new pairs of shoes, it makes them feel better about themselves. In many cases, this may be the first pair of shoes that the child has ever owned. In most cases, it is the first *new* clothing the child has ever owned. In either situation, what this does for a child is improve his or her self-esteem. Children are thrilled to be able to walk through their villages in their new shoes. It makes them feel that they have some worth. An increase in self-esteem is something that is not even measurable.

5   In conclusion, Mycoskie saw a need and established a company that is giving as much as it's getting in profits. So, when you purchase a pair of shoes from this company, you are not only giving to the company but also getting back the satisfaction of knowing that someone else is benefitting in many ways from your purchase.

1. What is the situation or cause that is described in this essay?

_____

2. Find the thesis statement of the essay. Write it below.

_____

3. What is the effect or result described in body paragraph 1?

_____

4. Write one detail or example that the writer used to support the first effect.

_____

5. What is the effect or result described in body paragraph 2?

_____

6. Write one detail or example that the writer used to support the second effect.

_____

7. What is the effect or result described in body paragraph 3?

_____

8. Write one detail or example that the writer used to support the third effect.

_____

iQ PRACTICE Go online for more practice with writing a cause/effect essay.
Practice › Unit 7 › Activity 10

Cause and effect: the sun makes plants grow

A **complex sentence** has an independent clause, or main clause, and one or more dependent clauses. A clause is a group of words that has a subject and a verb. An independent clause can stand alone as a complete sentence. A dependent clause cannot stand alone and must be used with a main clause. Dependent clauses that show cause can begin with subordinators like *because, since,* and *when.* Look at these examples.

> Lauren Bush Lauren founded the company FEED because she wanted to provide people with a way to help end hunger.
>
> When children are given a nutritious meal, they perform better in school.

The parts of the sentences beginning with *because, since,* and *when* are dependent clauses. If a dependent clause comes before the main clause, it is followed by a comma.

> dependent clause   main clause
>
> Because Bush Lauren had an interest in design, she was able to combine this
>
> with her desire to help hungry children.

A. IDENTIFY Underline the dependent clauses.

1. Their new computer repair business grew in the first year <u>because they all worked night and day</u>.

2. Since there was very little rain all spring, the amount of corn grown was very small.

3. When he invested $300 in the new company many years ago, he didn't know how much money he would make.

4. The school can now pick up many more children because someone donated another school bus.

5. They were able to finish building the house in a week since many volunteers came to help.

B. **APPLY** Combine the sentences using the words in parentheses. Add a comma where necessary.

1. Sammy saved all of the money he made in his summer job. He finally had enough money to buy a car. (because)

   <u>Because Sammy saved all of the money he made in his summer job,</u>
   <u>he finally had enough money to buy a car.</u>

2. The village no longer floods. The villagers planted a hundred trees on the hillside. (since)

   _____

   _____

3. The organization had received enough donations. It bought the new equipment. (when)

   _____

   _____

4. Mr. Kelly donated a great deal of money to the children's fund. He knew that the children needed a new school. (because)

   _____

   _____

5. People in the village suffered from extreme poverty. Many families could not afford to send their children to school. (since)

   _____

   _____

iQ PRACTICE Go online for more practice with complex sentences.
Practice › Unit 7 › Activities 11–12

UNIT ASSIGNMENT Write a cause/effect essay

OBJECTIVE ▶

In this assignment, you are going to write a cause/effect essay about how a business can earn money and do good. As you prepare to write, think about the Unit Question, "Can a business earn money while making a difference?" Use information from Reading 1, Reading 2, the unit video, and your work in this unit to support your paragraph. Refer to the Self-Assessment checklist on page 184.

iQ RESOURCES Go online to the Writing Tutor to read a model cause/effect essay. *Practice ⟩ Unit 7 ⟩ Activity 13*

PLAN AND WRITE

A. BRAINSTORM Work in a group. Brainstorm situations in which a business can earn money and still do good. Think of the different companies and people who have done well and done good for society at the same time. What was the problem that they wanted to address? How did they address it?

B. PLAN Choose one of the situations from Activity A. List at least three effects or results of this situation.

1. _____

2. _____

3. _____

iQ RESOURCES Go online to download and complete the outline for your cause/effect essay. *Resources ⟩ Writing Tools ⟩ Unit 7 ⟩ Outline*

C. WRITE Use your planning notes to write your essay.

1. Write your cause/effect essay.

2. Look at the Self-Assessment checklist on page 184 to guide your writing.

iQ PRACTICE Go online to the Writing Tutor to write your assignment. *Practice ⟩ Unit 7 ⟩ Activity 14*

REVISE AND EDIT

iQ RESOURCES Go online to download the peer review worksheet.
Resources > Writing Tools > Unit 7 > Peer Review Worksheet

A. PEER REVIEW Read your partner's essay. Then use the peer review worksheet (*Resource > Unit 7 > Pear Review*). Discuss the review with your partner.

B. REWRITE Based on your partner's review, revise and rewrite your essay.

C. EDIT Complete the Self-Assessment checklist as you prepare to write the final draft of your essay. Be prepared to hand in your work or discuss it in class.

SELF-ASSESSMENT	Yes	No
Does the Introductory paragraph contain a thesis statement?	☐	☐
Does the introductory paragraph describe the situation (cause) and its effects?	☐	☐
Does the essay include three body paragraphs that each describe an effect?	☐	☐
Does the essay include a concluding paragraph that summarizes the situation (cause) and its effects?	☐	☐
Does the essay include complex sentences? If not, where could one or two be added?	☐	☐
Does the essay include collocations with verbs? If not, where could one or two be added?	☐	☐
Does the essay include vocabulary from the unit?	☐	☐
Did you check the essay for punctuation, spelling, and grammar?	☐	☐

D. REFLECT Discuss these questions with a partner or group.

1. What is something new you learned in this unit?

2. Look back at the Unit Question—Can a business earn money while making a difference? Is your answer different now than it was when you started the unit? If yes, how is it different? Why?

iQ PRACTICE Go to the online discussion board to discuss the questions.
Practice > Unit 7 > Activity 15

TRACK YOUR SUCCESS

iQ PRACTICE Go to the online to check the words and phrases you have learned in the unit. *Practice > Unit 7 > Activity 16*

Check (✓) the skills and strategies you learned. If you need more work on a skill, refer to the page(s) in parentheses.

READING	☐ I can use a timeline. (p. 165)
CRITICAL THINKING	☐ I can add details to my writing to support a statement. (p. 174)
VOCABULARY	☐ I can use collocations with verbs. (p. 176)
WRITING	☐ I can write a cause/effect essay. (p. 177)
GRAMMAR	☐ I can use complex sentences. (p. 181)
OBJECTIVE ▶	☐ I can gather information and ideas to write a cause/effect essay about how a business can earn money and do good.

8 Behavioral Studies

READING	scanning a text
CRITICAL THINKING	identifying problems and solutions
VOCABULARY	collocations with adjectives + prepositions
WRITING	writing an argumentative essay
GRAMMAR	sentence fragments

UNIT QUESTION

What does it take to be successful?

A. Discuss these questions with your classmates.

1. How does someone become a successful athlete?

2. What are some things people give up or sacrifice in order to be successful?

3. Look at the photo. What do you think these women needed to do in order to be successful?

B. Listen to *The Q Classroom* online. Then answer these questions.

1. Felix believes success does not have to be about money or a career. How can a person be successful without earning a lot of money?

2. Sophy believes that people can't be successful by themselves. Do you agree or disagree? Why?

3. Marcus states that people need to be able to adapt to changes in order to be successful. Do you feel the same way? Can you give an example?

iQ PRACTICE Go to the online discussion board to discuss the Unit Question with your classmates. *Practice > Unit 8 > Activity 1*

UNIT OBJECTIVE

Read the articles and gather information and ideas to write an argumentative essay about what it takes to be successful.

READING 1

OBJECTIVE ▶

Fast Cars, Big Money

You are going to read an article from a business magazine about the popular sport of car racing, written from a business perspective. Use the article to gather information and ideas for your Unit Assignment.

PREVIEW THE READING

A. PREVIEW Read the headings. What do you think is the purpose of the article? Check (✓) your answer.

☐ to explain the sport of Formula 1 car racing

☐ to encourage businesses to invest in car racing

☐ to compare Formula 1 car races around the world

☐ to show why car racing is an expensive sport

B. QUICK WRITE What are some ways businesses attract more customers? Write for 5–10 minutes in response. Be sure to use this section for your Unit Assignment.

C. VOCABULARY Check (✓) the words you know. Then work with a partner to locate each word in the reading. Use clues to help define the words you don't know. Check your definitions in the dictionary.

assured *(adj.)*	invest *(v.)* 🔑	profit *(n.)* 🔑
dependable *(adj.)*	logo *(n.)*	sponsor *(v.)* 🔑
expansion *(n.)* OPAL	market *(n.)* 🔑	stability *(n.)* OPAL
image *(n.)* 🔑 OPAL		

🔑 Oxford 3000™ words   **OPAL** Oxford Phrasal Academic Lexicon

iQ PRACTICE Go online to listen and practice your pronunciation.
Practice ⟩ Unit 8 ⟩ Activity 2

WORK WITH THE READING

 A. INVESTIGATE Read the article and gather information about what it takes to be successful.

FAST CARS, BIG MONEY

DOES YOUR BUSINESS NEED A BOOST?

1   Imagine 350 million people seeing your company **logo** every year. Imagine this number growing even higher every year. Imagine being part of one of the most prestigious[1] and glamorous[2] sports in the world and making millions of dollars at the same time. Sound attractive? Hundreds of companies have already discovered the financial benefits of **sponsoring** Formula 1 racing. When you choose to sponsor a team, you can be **assured** that your company will grow financially and globally.

WHY ARE COMPANIES INTERESTED?

2   Companies have realized that investments in the sport of auto racing can bring them huge **profits**. Businesses, including banks, hotels, and telecommunication companies, **invest** tens of millions of dollars every year to sponsor race teams. Hundreds of millions of people watch car races every year. For companies, this is an enormous **market**.

3   Cars race around the track with company logos stuck to the doors, hood, and trunk, and people notice. Corporate sponsors can invest $5 million in a race team and make $30 million or more from car advertising. These costs are cheap compared to the profits. Sponsoring a team also shows the financial **stability** of your company. Race cars can cost tens of millions of dollars, and race teams can spend up to $300 million a year. Companies who invest in race teams are showing the world that they are powerful and **dependable**.

WHY IS INVESTING NOW A GOOD IDEA?

4   Much of Formula 1's current success comes from its **expansion** to global markets. Although most races are in Europe, today there are races in the Middle East and Asia. Companies support worldwide expansion because it gives them new customers in emerging markets. They can push their brand[3] globally. Many companies have already invested in Formula 1's most recent host locations, including Bahrain, Abu Dhabi, and Singapore. As a result, they have been able to expand their business to the Middle East and

Formula 1 race car

---

[1] **prestigious:** respected or admired because of success

[2] **glamorous:** attractive or full of glamor

[3] **brand:** the name of a product that is made by a particular company

Asia. These areas of the world are full of business opportunities, 3-C
and Formula 1 racing has brought them more growth and success.
Expanding overseas also shows that your company has a global 4-C
message, which is important in today's global economy.

WHY SHOULD MY COMPANY INVEST?

5   Thanks to a strong business mentality, Formula 1 racing has
become a profitable sport for corporations to invest in. The global
economy is always changing, but the industry has succeeded by
finding new ways to make more money. Sponsoring a team will
not only bring your company profits, but will also improve your
company's **image** as a business that is stable and globally-minded. 4-C
Take advantage of this wonderful business opportunity and enjoy
being part of this glamorous, thrill-seeking⁴ sport. Vroom vroom!

⁴ **thrill-seeking:** trying to find pleasure in excitement

B. VOCABULARY Here are some words from Reading 1. Read the sentences.
Circle the word or phrase that can replace the bold word without changing
the meaning of the sentence.

1. A company **logo** often gives the full name of the company or the first letter of
   the name. *symbol* / *address* / *rule*

2. Many companies regularly **sponsor** sports teams so that they can put
   advertising on their uniforms. *support* / *watch* / *buy*

3. A brand-new business cannot be **assured** that it will succeed right away.
   worried / *sure* / *interested*

4. Businesses need to make a **profit** consistently in order to be successful.
   income / *friends* / *decisions*

5. When companies **invest** money to make a new product, they have to consider
   the costs carefully. *need* / *lose* / *spend*

6. The Internet has given businesses access to a bigger **market** around
   the world. *number of customers* / *number of difficulties* / *number of computers*

7. Large companies generally have more **stability** than small businesses.
   choice / *strength* / *problems*

8. It is wise to invest in **dependable** companies because they tend to manage their
   money well. *new* / *reliable* / *different*

9. There has been a large **expansion** in the number of bilingual jobs because of
   the global economy. *decrease* / *growth* / *cost*

10. In order to be successful, a business needs to consider its **image**, or the way the
    public sees it. *attitude* / *appearance* / *growth*

iQ PRACTICE Go online for more practice with the vocabulary.
Practice > Unit 8 > Activity 3

C. IDENTIFY Read the main ideas. Write the paragraph number where they are found.

better F

5-1 1. By sponsoring a Formula 1 team, a company will grow financially and globally.

5-③ 2. Formula 1 sponsorship is profitable and shows that a company is powerful and reliable.

2 3. Sponsors can make a lot of money from car advertising.

4 4. Formula 1 racing is a good investment today because of its expansion to global markets.

5 5. Sponsorship brings companies profits and improves their image.

WRITING TIP

Activity E asks you to write a summary using the graphic organizer in Activity D. Use a graphic organizer before you write a summary to help you see how the ideas in a text are organized.

D. CATEGORIZE Work with a partner or group. Complete the graphic organizer for Reading 1. List two reasons that answer each question.

	Reason 1	Reason 2
1. Why are companies interested in Formula 1 racing?	Companies can make huge profits.	That shows the financial stability of the company. Paragraph 3 - 2
2. Why is investing in Formula 1 racing now a good idea?	because there are racing around the world now and companies can push their brand globally	It shows that a company has a global message.
3. Why should companies invest in Formula 1 racing?	because racing is and Popular in middle east and Asia now and there are a lot of business	racing is a profitable sport improve image

opportunities in these countries

E. COMPOSE Write a summary of Reading 1. Use the graphic organizer in Activity D to help you write your summary.

WRITING TIP

Activity F asks you to identify what the words *this* and *these* refer to in a previous sentence. Writers use *this* and *these* to continue an idea in a following sentence. Use *this* for a singular noun. Use *these* for a plural noun.

F. IDENTIFY Read these sentences from Reading 1. Then answer the questions. Find the sentences in the reading to help you.

1. (Paragraph 1) Imagine **this** number growing even higher every year.

   What number does *this* refer to? _number of people (350 millions)_

2. (Paragraph 2) For companies, **this** is an enormous market.

   What market does *this* refer to? _Hundred of millions of people_

3. (Paragraph 3) **This** cost is cheap compared to the profits.

   What costs does *this* refer to? _5 millions_

4. (Paragraph 4) **These** areas of the world are full of business opportunities.

   What areas of the world does *these* refer to? ~~middle east and Asia~~

5. (Paragraph 5) Take advantage of **this** wonderful business opportunity and enjoy being part of **this** glamorous, thrill-seeking sport.

   a. What business opportunity does *this* refer to? Sponsering a team

   b. What sport does *this* refer to? racing

iQ PRACTICE Go online for additional reading and comprehension.
Practice > Unit 8 > Activity 4

WRITE WHAT YOU THINK

A. DISCUSS Discuss the questions in a group.

1. Is sponsoring Formula 1 racing a good or bad investment? Explain.

2. Do you think that businesses that sponsor sports like car racing would be as successful without giving sponsorship money? Why or why not?

3. Why do you think banks choose to advertise on Formula 1 racing cars?

B. COMPOSE Choose one of the questions from Activity A and write a paragraph in response. Look back at your Quick Write on page 188 as you think about what you learned.

READING SKILL Scanning a text

Scanning means looking through a text quickly to find specific information, such as names, numbers, and dates. We scan items like the newspaper, a timetable, a dictionary, and the table of contents in a book. When you scan, do not read every word. Look for key words or phrases that will help you find the answer quickly. Think about how the information will appear on the page. For example, if you are looking for a date, scan only for numbers.

A. APPLY Scan Reading 1 for the missing information. Use key words in the sentences to help you find the answers. Then complete each statement.

Name of company

(places / location a car)

1. Businesses that sponsor race teams include ___bank___, ___hotels___, and ___telecomunication___.

2. Company logos are stuck to the ___door___, ___hood___, and ___trunk___ of race cars.

3. Although most Formula 1 races are in Europe, today there are races in ___middle east___ and ___asia___.

Name of races

B. **IDENTIFY** Scan Reading 1 again for the missing numbers. Use key words in the sentences to help you find the answers. Then complete each statement.

[margin notes: Number, money, money, money]

1. Every year, _____350_____ million people watch Formula 1 races.

2. Businesses invest _____tens_____ of _____million_____ of dollars every year to sponsor race teams.

3. Corporate sponsors can invest just _____5 million_____ in a race team and make _____30 million_____ or more.

4. Race teams can spend up to _____300_____ a year.

iQ PRACTICE Go online for more practice with scanning a text.
Practice > Unit 8 > Activity 5

READING 2

Practice Makes . . . Pain?

OBJECTIVE ▶

You are going to read a newspaper article about child athletes and what they do to succeed in sports. Use the article to gather information and ideas for your Unit Assignment.

PREVIEW THE READING

A. **PREVIEW** Look at the title. What do you think the writer will say about child athletes? Check (✓) your answer.

☐ It's easy for children to be successful in sports if they start early.

☐ The sacrifices children make for success in sports are sometimes too great.

WRITING TIP
Remember to use reasons to explain the main idea in your topic sentence.

B. **QUICK WRITE** Are competitive sports good for children? Write for 5–10 minutes in response. Include a topic sentence and supporting details. Be sure to use this section for your Unit Assignment.

C. **VOCABULARY** Check (✓) the words you know. Then work with a partner to locate each word in the reading.

aggressively *(adv.)*	due to *(prep. phr.)* OPAL	recover *(v.)* 🔑
dedication *(n.)*	exception *(n.)* OPAL	sign *(n.)* 🔑
demanding *(adj.)*	motion *(n.)*	trend *(n.)* 🔑 OPAL

🔑 Oxford 3000™ words   OPAL Oxford Phrasal Academic Lexicon

iQ PRACTICE Go online to listen and practice your pronunciation.
Practice > Unit 8 > Activity 6

WORK WITH THE READING

🔊 **A. INVESTIGATE** Read the article and gather information about what it takes to be successful.

PRACTICE MAKES ... PAIN

1   At ten, Courtney Thompson was a top-ranked gymnast in New Hampshire. She had been doing flips since she was one and had her heart set on competing in the Olympics. She practiced four and a half hours a day, six days a week, often repeating the same move 100 times. Her **demanding** schedule took a toll[1]. It got to the point where Courtney could barely straighten her elbows unless she put ice on them. On January 12, 2005, she had to stop in the middle of a floor routine. "I jumped up and grabbed my arm. It hurt really bad."

2   Doctors discovered that Courtney's constant workouts had caused the cartilage, or connective tissue, in her elbow to separate from the bone. She had surgery on both arms and went through months of painful rehabilitation[2]. Courtney's experience is part of a growing **trend** in youth sports—kids and teens were starting to have the same type of injuries that only professional athletes used to have. Experts say kids are pushing their bodies to the limit, practicing sports too hard for too long. The exhausting schedules often lead to dangerous injuries that could keep young athletes from competing—permanently.

◎ Under Strain

3   According to experts at *The Physician and Sportsmedicine* journal, between 30 and 50 percent of youth sports injuries are **due to** overuse. Overuse injuries are caused by repetitive **motion** that, over time, puts more stress on a body part than it can handle. The tissue or bone eventually breaks, stretches, or tears.

4   Danny Clark ended up with an overuse injury last year. The teen baseball player from Altamonte Springs, Florida, hurt himself by throwing 80 pitches in a single game after two months of not pitching at all. The sudden repetitive action tore Danny's rotator cuff. The rotator cuff is a group of four muscles and the tendons that connect them to bones in the shoulder. Afterward, he couldn't pitch

[1] **take a toll:** to have a negative effect
[2] **rehabilitation:** the process of returning to a normal life again after an injury

for two months and needed five months of physical therapy.

◉ Too Much, Too Soon (too young)

5 Experts say injuries such as Danny's are on the rise, in part because more and more kids are leaving casual sports for organized team competitions that require hours of practice and game time. "Kids [are] playing sports more **aggressively** at younger ages," explains James Beaty, an orthopedist in Memphis, Tennessee.

6 Kevin Butcher, a 15-year-old soccer player from Fort Collins, Colorado, is no **exception**. He plays soccer three or four times a week for nine months a year. His **dedication** pays off—last year he helped lead his team to a state championship. But his success came with a price. "Last year, I sprained my ankle a few times, dislocated³ a bone in my foot, and broke both sides of my pelvis⁴," Kevin says. The first time he broke his pelvis, Kevin didn't realize it for about a month. He played through the pain until doctors forced him to rest. When he dislocated a bone in his foot, a physical therapist put the bone into place, bandaged his foot, and let him play the next day.

◉ Knowing Your Limits

7 Not every kid who plays sports ends up with serious injuries. Experts say the key to avoiding injury is paying attention to your body. Feeling sore after practice is OK, but sharp pain is a warning **sign** that shouldn't be ignored. Kevin learned that lesson while **recovering** from his second broken pelvis in less than a year. "There's definitely a glory in playing through pain, but I think there is a limit. You just have to know when to stop."

³ **dislocate:** to put a bone out of its correct position
⁴ **pelvis:** the set of wide bones at the bottom of your back that connect to your legs

---

B. VOCABULARY Here are some words from Reading 2. Read the sentences. Circle the word or phrase that can replace the bold word without changing the meaning. Then compare your answers with a partner.

1. Ice skating is a **demanding** sport that requires a lot of time, practice, and hard work.

   a. difficult   b. expensive   c. harmful

2. Putting kids in sports at a young age is a growing **trend** in many countries today.

   a. new profession   b. general change   c. high cost

3. We canceled the soccer game **due to** the pouring rain. It was too wet and dangerous to play.

   a. because of   b. in order to   c. late for

4. The official made a **motion** with his hand to let the runners know it was time to start the race.

   a. ticket   b. question   (c.) movement

5. Athletes who play sports **aggressively** get hurt more frequently than athletes who don't.

   (a.) forcefully   b. quietly   c. quickly

6. Most competitive athletes earn money for playing sports, but gymnasts are an **exception**. They do not receive a salary.

   a. new rule   (b.) someone not included   c. professional athlete

7. Competitive athletes must have **dedication** because it takes a lot of time and hard work to be successful in sports.

   a. money   b. skill   (c.) commitment

8. Sore, aching muscles are a warning **sign** that you have exercised very hard.

   (a.) signal   b. injury   c. sacrifice

9. It can take months for an athlete to **recover** from a serious injury.

   a. compete   b. get sick   (c.) get better

iQ PRACTICE   Go online for more practice with the vocabulary.
Practice > Unit 8 > Activity 7

C. EXPLAIN Answer the questions. Write the paragraph number where the answer is found. Then discuss your answers with a partner.

1. What are many youth sport injuries due to? Paragraph: _3_

   _____ overuse _____

2. What causes an overuse injury? Paragraph: _3_

   _____

3. Why do children in youth sports have more injuries today? Paragraph: _2_

   _____

4. Why do organized team competitions cause more injuries? Paragraph: _2_

   _____

5. How can child athletes avoid injury? Paragraph: _7_

   _____

D. CATEGORIZE Scan Reading 2. Complete the chart with the missing information.

TIP FOR SUCCESS

Activity D asks you to complete a **chart**. A chart is a graphic organizer readers use to see relationships between ideas. Identifying relationships between ideas in a text will help you become a more effective reader.

Name	Home	Sport	Injury
1. Courtney Thompson	New Hampshire	*gymnast*	*straighten her elbows*
2. *Danny Clark*	*Altamonte Springs, Florida*	baseball	*tendons in shoulder*
3. *Kevin Butcher*	*Colorado*	*soccer*	sprained ankle, dislocated bone, broken pelvis

E. CATEGORIZE Read the statements. Write *F* (fact) or *O* (opinion).

F 1. Courtney Thompson practiced gymnastics six days a week.

F 2. Between 30 and 50 percent of youth sports injuries are due to overuse.

F 3. Overuse injuries are caused by physical stress on tissue or bone.

O 4. Child athletes are playing sports too hard for too long.

F 5. The number of overuse injuries in children is increasing.

O 6. Soccer player Kevin Butcher showed a lot of dedication.

F 7. Kevin Butcher's soccer team won the state championship last year.

O 8. Listening to your body is an important lesson for athletes to learn.

CRITICAL THINKING STRATEGY

Identifying problems and solutions

Writers often **present a problem** as the topic of a reading and then **offer solutions** for the problem. When you read, first identify what the main problem is. Then read through the whole text to find all the solutions.

Next, evaluate the solutions: do you think they solve the problem? What are their disadvantages? Finally, brainstorm alternative solutions to see if there are better ways to solve the problem. Use personal evidence or evidence from the text to justify your opinions.

iQ PRACTICE Go online to watch the Critical Thinking Video and check your comprehension. *Practice > Unit 8 > Activity 8*

F. IDENTIFY Look back at Reading 2 to identify the main problem and the solutions. Complete the graphic organizer. Then discuss the questions with a partner.

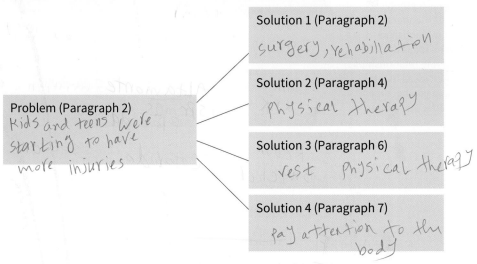

Problem (Paragraph 2)
Kids and teens were starting to have more injuries

Solution 1 (Paragraph 2)
surgery, rehabillation

Solution 2 (Paragraph 4)
physical therapy

Solution 3 (Paragraph 6)
rest physical therapy

Solution 4 (Paragraph 7)
pay attention to the body

1. Which solution do you think is the best solution? Why?

2. What other solutions can you think of? Are they better solutions than the ones mentioned in the text? Explain.

G. INTERPRET Check (✓) the statements you can infer from the reading.

☐ 1. Overuse injuries are usually permanent.

☑ 2. Fewer children had overuse injuries in the past. (we have trend now)

☐ 3. Overuse injuries happen more often to soccer players than baseball players.

☑ 4. It can take children months to recover from an overuse injury.

☐ 5. Parents do not want their children to play casual sports anymore.

☑ 6. It is normal for child athletes to feel sore after they practice sports.

☑ 7. Sharp pain can be a warning sign of an overuse injury.

☐ 8. Young athletes are more at risk of injuring themselves than older athletes are.

H. COMPOSE Why do you think some athletes like to "push through their pain" instead of quitting? Write a paragraph of 5–8 sentences giving your opinion.

I. DISCUSS Discuss the questions in a group. Look back at your Quick Write on page 193 as you think about what you learned.

1. Do you think competing in sports is good for young children? Explain.

2. Do you think coaches and parents have a responsibility to try to stop children from getting hurt while doing sports? Why or why not?

WORK WITH THE VIDEO

A. PREVIEW Should universities give athletes money so that they can attend college? Share your opinion with a partner.

iQ RESOURCES Go online to watch the video about sports at Arizona State University. *Resources > Video > Unit 8 > Unit Video*

B. IDENTIFY Watch the video two or three times. Then answer the questions.

1. How many students attend Arizona State?

   _____

2. What sport did Ike Davis play at Arizona State?

   _____

3. What is the average annual cost for a student at Arizona State?

   _____

4. How does Arizona State attract top athletes?

   _____

5. Why do American universities invest in sports?

   _____

C. EXTEND Do you think universities should spend lots of money on sports facilities like stadiums, pools, and golf courses? Why or why not? Write a paragraph of 5–8 sentences in response.

? WRITE WHAT YOU THINK

SYNTHESIZE Think about Reading 1, Reading 2, and the unit video as you discuss these questions. Then choose one question and write a paragraph in response.

1. What are some ways that athletes pay for success?

2. How do parents of child athletes pay for success? Consider financial, physical, and psychological costs in your response.

VOCABULARY SKILL Collocations with adjectives + prepositions

Collocations are words that frequently go together. One common pattern for collocations is adjective + preposition.

Adjective + Preposition		Adjective + Preposition	
interested	in	famous	for
due	to	upset	about

Learning collocations will help you increase your vocabulary and improve your writing.

iQ RESOURCES Go online to watch the Vocabulary Skill Video.
Resources > Video > Unit 8 > Vocabulary Skill Video

ACADEMIC LANGUAGE

The corpus shows that *due to* is more common in academic writing than academic speaking.

_____ **OPAL**
Oxford Phrasal Academic Lexicon

A. APPLY Complete the sentences with the adjective + preposition collocations from the box.

afraid of	famous for ⁵	involved in ⁶	sure about ³
due to ²	interested in ⁷	nervous about ⁸	upset about ⁴

1. Parents whose children compete in sports are often _afraid of_ injuries.

2. The player's injury was _____ overuse.

3. Carlos was not _____ about the rules of the game, so he asked his coach.

4. Felix was very _____ losing the championship game. He really wanted to win.

5. Nadia Comăneci is _____ being one of the greatest gymnasts in history.

6. More children are _____ organized sports at a very young age today. My neighbor's son started playing soccer when he was four.

7. Are you _____ going to the baseball game tonight? I have an extra ticket if you'd like to go.

8. The gymnast was _____ competing for the first time in front of hundreds of people.

B. COMPOSE Choose five adjective + preposition collocations from Activity A. Write a sentence using each collocation.

1. _____

   _____

2. _____

   _____

3. _____

   _____

4. _____

   _____

5. _____

   _____

iQ PRACTICE Go online for more practice with using collocations with adjectives + prepositions. *Practice > Unit 8 > Activity 9*

WRITING

OBJECTIVE ▶

At the end of this unit, you will write an argumentative essay about what it takes to be successful. This essay will include specific information from the readings, the unit video, and your own ideas.

WRITING SKILL Writing an argumentative essay

An **argumentative essay** expresses how the writer feels about a topic. For example, it might express whether the writer agrees or disagrees with an idea.

The introductory paragraph in an argumentative essay includes the thesis statement, which clearly states the writer's opinion or view about a topic. The introductory paragraph may include background information and a **counterargument** to the writer's opinion. A counterargument is the opposite opinion. Writers sometimes mention a counterargument and then explain why it's not true in order to make their point stronger.

Each body paragraph of an argumentative essay includes a topic sentence that states a reason for the writer's opinion. Examples or facts are given to support each reason.

The concluding paragraph of an argumentative essay restates the opinion and refers to the counterargument. The concluding paragraph also summarizes the reasons the writer has this opinion. Often, the concluding paragraph includes an additional idea, sometimes a prediction, about the topic.

TIP FOR SUCCESS

Writers use certain phrases to introduce a counterargument, such as *some people say that, some people think that,* and *some people argue that.*

A. WRITING MODEL Read the model argumentative essay. Then answer the questions on pages 203–204.

Competitive Soccer: An Ideal Sport for Children

Soccer is the most popular sport in the world, and for many people, it is an important part of their childhood. Many children join competitive soccer leagues at a very young age. Some parents, however, believe that competitive soccer is too dangerous. They worry about their children getting a serious injury, so they decide to put them in a less aggressive team sport like basketball or baseball. I don't think this is a good enough reason not to let children play soccer. The fact is that children can get injured playing any sport. Even baseball players can get serious injuries. If children aren't allowed to join competitive soccer leagues, I believe they will miss out on very important advantages of playing this wonderful sport. Soccer is an ideal sport for children, and as a competitive soccer player, a child will not only get a good physical workout, but will also learn valuable lessons about teamwork and discipline.

First, playing competitive soccer keeps children in good shape. Soccer players build strength, flexibility, and endurance. Unlike some sports, soccer requires children to move around constantly. This constant motion helps players build muscles and burn fat more efficiently. Running not only strengthens leg muscles, but also burns a lot of calories, and it improves heart health. Children who play less active competitive sports, like baseball, do not enjoy these same advantages because they can spend long stretches of time just standing around.

Second, being a competitive soccer player teaches children the importance of teamwork. A soccer team has 11 players and several positions. Forwards score goals, fullbacks and goalies defend, and halfbacks assist both forwards and fullbacks. All of these players depend on each other during a game. Therefore, they have to learn to communicate well, and they must trust one another if they want to win. Learning teamwork, good communication skills, and trust will not just help children succeed on a competitive soccer team. The truth is these skills and values will also be useful in their lives at home, at school, and eventually, into adulthood.

Finally, competitive soccer is one of the best ways for children to learn about discipline. Players often practice after school or early in the morning, and they have games on the weekend. Young soccer players, however, also have to worry about completing all their schoolwork. In order to do both successfully, children learn how to manage their time effectively to meet homework deadlines and to show up to soccer practice on time. Competitive players also have to take good care of themselves by eating healthy food and keeping their bodies in good shape, which teaches them self-control.

There are still parents out there who will not put their children in competitive soccer because of the risk of injury. However, I believe this wonderful sport actually has many advantages over other sports. These children are often in excellent shape, and most importantly, they are learning values and skills that they will carry with them into adulthood, like discipline and teamwork. As long as parents monitor their children, they can help to make sure they avoid possible injury, and in that case, everybody wins.

1. Look at the introductory paragraph. What is the counterargument? Circle it. Which sentence states the writer's opinion about the topic? Underline it.

2. Look at the body paragraphs. What are the three reasons that the writer gives for his or her opinion?

Reason 1: _____

_____

Reason 2: _____

_____

Reason 3: _____

_____

3. Look at the concluding paragraph. Which sentence refers to the counterargument? Circle it. Which sentence restates the writer's opinion? Underline it.

4. What additional idea does the writer include in the concluding paragraph? Why do you think the writer added this idea?

_____

_____

TIP FOR SUCCESS

Activity B asks you to give your opinion about something you've read. When you state whether you agree or disagree with an author, include reasons for your opinion so that your ideas are well supported.

B. COMPOSE Look again at the model essay in Activity A. Do you agree or disagree with the writer? Write a paragraph of 5–8 sentences giving your opinion. Include reasons to support your opinion.

C. WRITING MODEL Read the essay question. Then read the introductory paragraph and first body paragraph of the model argumentative essay. Answer the questions on page 205.

Essay question: *Should parents let their child athletes leave home at an early age so they can train for the Olympics?*

Experts agree that child athletes are training harder and longer than they did in the past. Compared to before, children today who take up competitive sports, like figure skating or gymnastics, train so seriously that many leave home at a young age to follow their dream. In fact, gymnasts as young as eight years old may leave home and live far away to train with the best coaches. This is because many parents believe good coaches will give their children the opportunity to compete in the Olympics one day, and it is worth the sacrifice. However, I believe sending athletes away from home so young is not the right choice. Parents of these young competitive athletes should not let them leave home to train for the Olympics for three important reasons.

First of all, parents should not let their children leave home to train because they lose precious time with them. Children will not live with their parents forever. The years they spend with their parents go very quickly. One day they're in kindergarten, and the next day it seems like they're off to college. Sending children away may make them better athletes, but it cannot replace this lost time together. For example, they won't be able to read together every night or go shopping together whenever they want. Parents could also miss out on important events, like birthdays or the first day at a new school. I think parents will regret their decision when their children are grown up and they have missed these important days and events.

1. Circle the sentence in the introductory paragraph that states the counterargument.

2. Underline the sentence in the introductory paragraph that gives the writer's opinion about the topic.

3. What reason does the writer give to support his or her opinion? Circle the sentence in the body paragraph that states the reason.

4. The writer states, "Sending children away may make them better athletes, but it cannot replace **this lost time** together." What does this lost time refer to?

_____

5. What examples does the writer use to support his or her reason in the body paragraph?

Example 1: <u>not able to read together every night</u>

Example 2: _____

Example 3: _____

Example 4: _____

6. Do you think the writer's first reason is convincing? Why or why not? Share your answer with a partner.

WRITING TIP
Activity D asks you to provide examples. Writers often use *for example* and *for instance* to signal examples. *For example* and *for instance* usually begin a new sentence and are followed by a comma.

D. COMPOSE Read the topic sentence for a second body paragraph for the essay assignment in Activity C. Write 5–8 supporting sentences for the paragraph. Include examples to support the reason in the topic sentence.

Second, parents who send their children to train far away from home will not be able to be around when their children need them. For example,

E. EVALUATE Read this concluding paragraph for the essay assignment in Activity C. Then answer the questions.

1. Which sentence refers to the counterargument? Circle it.

Many parents think letting their child athlete train far away from home is a good idea because it will help them compete in the Olympics one day.

However, they also have to think about the consequences. I think parents will regret their decision later on because they will have missed out on important days and events in their children's lives, as well as moments when their children really needed them by their side. In addition, parents could be wasting their money, since only a small number of athletes make it to the Olympics, even if they show a lot of potential at a young age. For these three reasons, parents need to think very hard before making a decision that could negatively affect their lives and their children's lives for years to come.

2. Which sentence restates the writer's opinion and summarizes the first two reasons? Underline it.

3. According to the conclusion, what was the topic of the third body paragraph?

_____

_____

4. What prediction does the writer make at the end of the conclusion?

_____

_____

5. Do you agree or disagree with the writer's prediction? Why? Share your answer with a partner.

iQ PRACTICE   Go online for more practice with writing an argumentative essay. *Practice > Unit 8 > Activity 10*

GRAMMAR Sentence fragments

A **sentence fragment** is an incomplete sentence that cannot stand alone. Sentence fragments are usually considered errors. It is important to avoid sentence fragments in your writing. Look at the examples.

> **Fragment:** When children play soccer.
> **Fragment:** Because children can get injured.

As you learned in Unit 7, these examples are **dependent clauses**. When used alone, they are fragments. They need to be combined with a main clause.

> <u>When children play soccer</u>, they learn the importance of teamwork.
> Parents worry about competitive sports <u>because children can get injured</u>.

Words such as *because*, *since*, *although*, *when*, or *after* are often used with dependent clauses. These words connect an incomplete sentence to a main clause to avoid a fragment.

A. CATEGORIZE Identify each sentence as a complete sentence (*S*) or a sentence fragment (*F*). Correct the sentence fragments with a partner.

____ 1. When athletes feel pain.

____ 2. She always stretches for 20 minutes before she exercises.

____ 3. Because there are more children in competitive sports.

____ 4. Since I started playing soccer, I have lost weight.

____ 5. Although baseball looks easy to play.

B. APPLY Read the paragraph and correct any fragments.

I loved playing basketball in high school because it helped me make a lot of new friends. When I was young. I was a very shy person. It was difficult for me to speak with people. Because I was so shy. Then a classmate invited me to try out for the basketball team. I was pretty good, and I was picked for the team. Although I was nervous at first. I really enjoyed working with my teammates. We were like a family. We supported each other. When we played together against other schools. Many of us became good friends off the court, too. Little by little, I learned not to be so shy. Today I still keep in touch with my old teammates on social networking sites. Although we don't see each other anymore. We are still good friends. Thanks to them, I'm not shy like I used to be back in high school.

iQ PRACTICE Go online for more practice with sentence fragments.
Practice > Unit 8 > Activities 11–12

UNIT ASSIGNMENT

OBJECTIVE ▶

Write an argumentative essay

In this assignment, you are going to write an argumentative essay about what it takes to be successful. As you prepare your essay, think about the Unit Question, "What does it take to be successful?" Use information from Reading 1, Reading 2, the unit video, and your work in this unit to support your essay. Refer to the Self-Assessment checklist on page 209.

---

iQ PRACTICE Go online to the Writing Tutor to read a model argumentative essay. *Practice > Unit 8 > Activity 13*

PLAN AND WRITE

A. BRAINSTORM Follow these steps to help you organize your ideas.

1. Choose your topic from the box. Then look at the list of sports. Check (✓) the sport(s) you would like to discuss in your essay.

> Should athletes or sports teams accept money from corporate sponsors in order to be successful? Discuss one or more specific sports in your essay.
> Should child athletes be pushed hard in order to succeed? Discuss one or more specific sports in your essay.

- ☐ American football
- ☐ baseball
- ☐ basketball
- ☐ Formula 1 racing
- ☐ gymnastics
- ☐ rugby
- ☐ running
- ☐ soccer
- ☐ tennis
- ☐ (other) _____

2. Brainstorm reasons that will help support your opinion about the topic.

3. Brainstorm a counterargument for your essay. Why would someone disagree with your opinion?

B. PLAN Follow these steps to plan your essay.

1. Write a thesis statement for your essay that expresses your opinion about the topic. List your three best reasons from Activity A.

_____

_____

_____

2. Think about the readings and the unit video in this unit. Is there any information that can help support your ideas?

iQ RESOURCES Go online to download and complete the outline for your argumentative essay. *Resources > Writing Tools > Unit 8 > Outline*

C. WRITE Use your planning notes to write your essay.

1. Write your argumentative essay that explains what it takes to be successful. Be sure to use reasons and examples or facts to support your thesis statement.

2. Look at the Self-Assessment checklist on page 209 to guide your writing.

iQ PRACTICE Go online to the Writing Tutor to write your assignment. *Practice > Unit 8 > Activity 14*

REVISE AND EDIT

iQ RESOURCES Go online to download the peer review worksheet.
Resources > Writing Tools > Unit 8 > Peer Review Worksheet

A. PEER REVIEW Read your partner's essay. Then use the peer review worksheet. Discuss the review with your partner.

B. REWRITE Based on your partner's review, revise and rewrite your essay.

C. EDIT Complete the Self-Assessment checklist as you prepare to write the final draft of your essay. Be prepared to hand in your work or discuss it in class.

SELF-ASSESSMENT	Yes	No
Does the essay include an introductory paragraph that states an opinion and describes a counterargument?	☐	☐
Does the essay include three body paragraphs that each provide a reason and supporting examples or facts?	☐	☐
Does the essay contain a concluding paragraph that restates the opinion, refers to the counterargument, and summarizes the reasons?	☐	☐
Are there any sentence fragments? Underline them and then correct them.	☐	☐
Are adjective + preposition collocations used correctly?	☐	☐
Does the essay include vocabulary from the unit?	☐	☐
Did you check the essay for punctuation, spelling, and grammar?	☐	☐

D. REFLECT Discuss these questions with a partner or group.

1. What is something new you learned in this unit?

2. Look back at the Unit Question—What does it take to be successful? Is your answer different now than when you started the unit? If yes, how is it different? Why?

iQ PRACTICE Go to the online discussion board to discuss the questions.
Practice > Unit 8 > Activity 15

TRACK YOUR SUCCESS

iQ PRACTICE Go online to check the words and phrases you have learned in this unit. *Practice > Unit 8 > Activity 16*

Check (✓) the skills you learned. If you need more work on a skill, refer to the page(s) in parentheses.

READING ☐ I can scan a text. (p. 192)

CRITICAL THINKING ☐ I can identify problems and solutions. (p. 197)

VOCABULARY ☐ I can use collocations with adjectives + prepositions. (p. 200)

WRITING ☐ I can write an argumentative essay (p. 202)

GRAMMAR ☐ I can recognize and avoid sentence fragments. (p. 206)

OBJECTIVE ▶ ☐ I can gather information and ideas to write an argumentative essay about what it takes to be successful.

unintentionally = (adv), غیر عمدی = accidently

Legend = a traditinol story (true or not) (N)

nutual = متقابل (احساس) دو طرفه (adj)

ose = to create a threat, problem, etc
(V)

deteriorated = to become worse (bad)
(V) بدتر شدن

alongside = next to or the side of s/b or s/t
(adv)

deforestation: جنگل زدایی، بریدن، قطع کردن (N)

preserve = محافظت کردن (keep alive, safe)
(V)

extinct = منقرض (adj)

urgently (adv) با فوریت

vulnerable (adj) آسیب پذیر

microorganism (a very small living)
(N)

invasive (adj) متجاوز - مهاجم
(diseases spreading) very quickly

The **Oxford 3000**™ is a list of the 3,000 core words that every learner of English needs to know. The words have been chosen based on their frequency in the Oxford English Corpus and relevance to learners of English. Every word is aligned to the CEFR, guiding learners on the words they should know at the A1–B2 level.

OPAL The **Oxford Phrasal Academic Lexicon** is an essential guide to the most important words and phrases to know for academic English. The word lists are based on the Oxford Corpus of Academic English and the British Academic Spoken English corpus.

The **Common European Framework of Reference for Language (CEFR)** provides a basic description of what language learners have to do to use language effectively. The system contains 6 reference levels: A1, A2, B1, B2, C1, C2.

UNIT 1

accomplishment (n.) C1
authentic (adj.) C1
appreciate (v.) B1
consider (v.) OPAL A2
confidence (n.) B2
demonstrate (v.) OPAL B2
effective (adj.) OPAL B1
expect (v.) OPAL A2
impress (v.) B2
lead to (v. phr.) A2
maintain (v.) OPAL B2
offensive (adj.) B2
professional (adj.) OPAL A2
punctual (adj.) C1
research (n.) OPAL A2
responsible (adj.) OPAL B1
select (v.) OPAL B2
slang (n.) B2
stranger (n.) B1
weakness (n.) B2

UNIT 2

arrange (v.) B2
artistic (adj.) B2
at risk (prep. phr.) B1
balanced (adj.) OPAL B2
be made up of (v. phr.) B2
be willing to (v. phr.) B1

identical (adj.) OPAL B2
identify (v.) OPAL B2
influence (v.) OPAL B2
in terms of (prep. phr.) OPAL B1
likely (adj.) OPAL B1
method (n.) OPAL B1
occasion (n.) B1
principle (n.) OPAL B2
recognize (v.) OPAL B1
sensitive (adj.) OPAL B2
status symbol (n.) C1
system (n.) OPAL A2
typically (adv.) OPAL B1

UNIT 3

adapt (v.) OPAL B2
data (n.) OPAL A2
digital (adj.) OPAL A2
discover (v.) B1
feedback (n.) B2
global (adj.) OPAL B2
in favor of (prep. phr.) B1
interactive (adj.) OPAL C1
limitation (n.) OPAL B2
manufacturer (n.) B2
monitor (v.) OPAL C1
obey (v.) B2
obstacle (n.) B2
occur (v.) OPAL B2

reliable (adj.) OPAL B1
respond (v.) OPAL B2
revolutionize (v.) C1
sense (v.) OPAL B2
the benefits of (n. phr.) OPAL A2

UNIT 4

accurate (adj.) OPAL B1
acknowledge (v.) OPAL B2
annoying (adj.) B1
annual (adj.) OPAL B2
broadcasting (n.) B2
donation (n.) B2
entertain (v.) B1
exposure (n.) C1
factor (n.) OPAL A2
impact (n.) OPAL B1
imply (v.) OPAL B2
memorable (adj.) B2
reflect (v.) OPAL B2
relevant (adj.) OPAL B2
specifically (adv.) OPAL B1
suggest (v.) OPAL B2
support (v.) OPAL B1
surrounding (adj.) B2

UNIT 5

bravely *(adv.)* B1
conquer *(v.)* C1 ~~~ handwritten
determined *(adj.)* OPAL B1
distinctive *(adj.)* OPAL C1 *specific*
earn *(v.)* A2
element *(n.)* OPAL B1 *an important part of s/t*
emerge *(v.)* OPAL B2 *to appear unexpectedly*
enable *(v.)* OPAL B2
goal *(n.)* OPAL A2
perceive *(v.)* OPAL B2 *to see or think of particular way*
poverty *(n.)* OPAL B1
predict *(v.)* OPAL A2
role *(n.)* OPAL A2
set apart *(v. phr.)* C2
significant *(adj.)* OPAL B2
threat *(n.)* OPAL B2
trait *(n.)* B2 *make you sad*
traumatic *(adj.)* C1
ultimate *(adj.)* OPAL B2 *very good - top*

UNIT 6

according to *(prep.)* OPAL A2
arrogant *(adj.)* B2
come up with *(v. phr.)* B1 *create to find or produce an answer, money, etc*
complex *(adj.)* OPAL B2
deal with *(v. phr.)* A2 *solve a problem*
efficient *(adj.)* OPAL B1
experiment *(n.)* OPAL A2
function *(v.)* OPAL B2
have a gift *(v. phr.)* B2 *talent*
impatient *(adj.)* B2
make sense *(v. phr.)* A2
the meaning can be understood

move on *(v. phr.)* C1 *start s/t new*
pace *(n.)* B2
proof *(n.)* B2
rely on *(v. phr.)* B2 *to trust*
revolutionary *(adj.)* C1 *complete change*
subject *(n.)* OPAL C1 *a person*
view *(v.)* OPAL B1 *a personal opinion toward s/t*

UNIT 7

address *(v.)* OPAL B2 *manage, fix*
aspect *(n.)* OPAL B2
concerned *(adj.)* OPAL B2
desire *(n.)* OPAL B2
distribute *(v.)* OPAL B2
estimate *(v.)* OPAL B2 *calculate*
firsthand *(adv.)* C1 *heard, seen, learned directly*
focus *(n.)* OPAL A2
give back *(v. phr.)* B1 *to support*
inspired *(adj.)* B2
massive *(adj.)* B2
model *(n.)* OPAL A2
movement *(n.)* OPAL C1
opportunity *(n.)* OPAL B1 *a chance*
overall *(adj.)* OPAL B2 *including everything*
prospect *(n.)* B2
reusable *(adj.)* C1
seek *(v.)* OPAL B2
signify *(v.)* C1 *to be a sign of s/t, to mean*

(away don't waste money, time, energy)
(a scientific test that is done)

UNIT 8

aggressively *(adv.)* B2 *forcefully*
assured *(adj.)* C2 *sure*
dedication *(n.)* C1 *commitment*
demanding *(adj.)* B2 *demand, difficult*
dependable *(adj.)* C1 *reliable*
due to *(prep. phr.)* OPAL B1 *because of*
exception *(n.)* OPAL B2 *not include*
expansion *(n.)* OPAL B2 *groth*
image *(n.)* OPAL A2 *appearance*
invest *(v.)* B1 *spend*
logo *(n.)* B2 *symbol*
market *(n.)* B1 *number of customers*
motion *(n.)* B2 *movement*
profit *(n.)* B1 *income*
recover *(v.)* B2 *get better*
sign *(n.)* A2 *signal*
sponsor *(v.)* B2
stability *(n.)* OPAL C1 *strength*
trend *(n.)* OPAL B1 *general change*

Halloween
water
Alexa/smart tech
Vocab [Tanksgiving
Biodiversity

AUTHORS

Colin S. Ward is Chair of the Languages Department at Lone Star College-North Harris in Houston, Texas. He holds an M.A. in TESOL from the University of London and has been teaching English for over fifteen years. His interests include content-based language learning and the teaching of second-language writing. Colin is a U.S.-U.K. Fulbright scholar and the author of several ESL textbooks.

Margot F. Gramer holds an M.A. in TESOL from Teachers College, Columbia University. She has been involved in the field of ESL as a teacher, teacher-trainer, administrator, writer and editor. She has taught ESL for many years at both the college level and in business settings. She is the author or co-author of many ESL textbooks. She is currently an Instructor at the Language Immersion Program at Nassau Community College (LINCC) in Garden City, New York.

SERIES CONSULTANTS

Lawrence J. Zwier holds an M.A. in TESL from the University of Minnesota. He is currently the Associate Director for Curriculum Development at the English Language Center at Michigan State University in East Lansing. He has taught ESL/EFL in the United States, Saudi Arabia, Malaysia, Japan, and Singapore.

Marguerite Ann Snow holds a Ph.D. in Applied Linguistics from UCLA. She teaches in the TESOL M.A. program in the Charter College of Education at California State University, Los Angeles. She was a Fulbright scholar in Hong Kong and Cyprus. In 2006, she received the President's Distinguished Professor award at CSULA. She has trained ESL teachers in the United States and EFL teachers in more than 25 countries. She is the author/editor of numerous publications in the areas of content-based instruction, English for academic purposes, and standards for English teaching and learning. She is a co-editor of *Teaching English as a Second or Foreign Language* (4th ed.).

CRITICAL THINKING CONSULTANT **James Dunn** is a Junior Associate Professor at Tokai University and the Coordinator of the JALT Critical Thinking Special Interest Group. His research interests include Critical Thinking skills' impact on student brain function during English learning, as measured by EEG. His educational goals are to help students understand that they are capable of more than they might think and to expand their cultural competence with critical thinking and higher-order thinking skills.

ASSESSMENT CONSULTANT **Elaine Boyd** has worked in assessment for over 30 years for international testing organizations. She has designed and delivered courses in assessment literacy and is also the author of several EL exam coursebooks for leading publishers. She is an Associate Tutor (M.A. TESOL/Linguistics) at University College, London. Her research interests are classroom assessment, issues in managing feedback, and intercultural competences.

VOCABULARY CONSULTANT **Cheryl Boyd Zimmerman** is Professor Emeritus at California State University, Fullerton. She specialized in second-language vocabulary acquisition, an area in which she is widely published. She taught graduate courses on second-language acquisition, culture, vocabulary, and the fundamentals of TESOL, and has been a frequent invited speaker on topics related to vocabulary teaching and learning. She is the author of *Word Knowledge: A Vocabulary Teacher's Handbook* and Series Director of *Inside Reading, Inside Writing*, and *Inside Listening and Speaking* published by Oxford University Press.

ONLINE INTEGRATION **Chantal Hemmi** holds an Ed.D. TEFL and is a Japan-based teacher trainer and curriculum designer. Since leaving her position as Academic Director of the British Council in Tokyo, she has been teaching at the Center for Language Education and Research at Sophia University on an EAP/CLIL program offered for undergraduates. She delivers lectures and teacher trainings throughout Japan, Indonesia, and Malaysia.

COMMUNICATIVE GRAMMAR CONSULTANT **Nancy Schoenfeld** holds an M.A. in TESOL from Biola University in La Mirada, California, and has been an English language instructor since 2000. She has taught ESL in California and Hawaii, and EFL in Thailand and Kuwait. She has also trained teachers in the United States and Indonesia. Her interests include teaching vocabulary, extensive reading, and student motivation. She is currently an English Language Instructor at Kuwait University.